THE DEVILS AND EVIL SPIRITS OF BABYLONIA.

VOL. II

AMS PRESS
NEW YORK

Bronze animal-headed figure of one of the Babylonian Powers of Evil. The inscription upon it reads: (1) *Mu-kil pi* (?) (2) *-tik limuttim(tim)* (3) *ur-ru-ḫu* (4) *la-pit pagrâni*^{pl} (5) *mu-šar-bu* (6) *la-si-mu* (7) *la mu-ki-ia* (8) *ša aḫi*^{pl} (9) *šepâ* ^{II} *limuttim* (*tim*) (10) *iprus* (*us*). "He that raiseth an evil . . . , rushing headlong, upheaving the dead, exalting, galloping, never stopping, whose brothers stretch forth (?) feet for evil." (No. 93,078.)

(*Frontispiece.*)

THE

DEVILS AND EVIL SPIRITS

OF

BABYLONIA,

BEING BABYLONIAN AND ASSYRIAN INCANTATIONS AGAINST THE DEMONS, GHOULS, VAMPIRES, HOBGOBLINS, GHOSTS, AND KINDRED EVIL SPIRITS, WHICH ATTACK MANKIND.

TRANSLATED FROM THE ORIGINAL CUNEIFORM TEXTS IN THE BRITISH MUSEUM, WITH TRANSLITERATIONS, VOCABULARY, NOTES, ETC.

BY

R. CAMPBELL THOMPSON, M.A.

ASSISTANT IN THE DEPARTMENT OF EGYPTIAN AND ASSYRIAN ANTIQUITIES, BRITISH MUSEUM.

WITH TWO PLATES.

VOL. II.

"*FEVER SICKNESS*" *AND* "*HEADACHE,*" *ETC.*

London

LUZAC AND CO.

1904.

Library of Congress Cataloging in Publication Data

Thompson, Reginald Campbell, 1876-1941, tr.
The devils and evil spirits of Babylonia.

Reprint of the 1903-04 ed. published by Luzac, London, which was issued as v. 14-15 of Luzac's Semitic text and translation series.

CONTENTS: v. 1. Evil spirits.—v. 2. Fever sickness and headache.

1. Incantations, Assyro-Babylonian. 2. Assyro-Babylonian language—Texts. 3. Demonology, Assyro-Babylonian. I. Title. II. Series: Luzac's Semitic text and translation series; v. 14-15.

PJ3791.T5 1976 133.4′27 73-18855
ISBN 0-404-11353-2

Reprinted from an original copy in the collections of the Cleveland Public Library

From the edition of 1904, London
First AMS edition published in 1976
Manufactured in the United States of America

International Standard Book Number:
Complete Set: 0-404-11353-2
Volume II: 0-404-11355-9

AMS PRESS INC.
NEW YORK, N. Y. 10003

TO MY FATHER,

REGINALD E. THOMPSON, M.D.

Preface.

THE Series of Cuneiform Texts which are transliterated and translated in this, the second volume of my work on the Devils and Evil Spirits of Babylonia, are of a magical character, except for the interesting descriptions which are given of supernatural beings which form the concluding portion of the book. In contents, construction, and phraseology they closely resemble the documents relating to Evil Spirits, which will be found in the preceding volume.

A careful examination of the documents makes it almost certain that they were originally written in the ancient non-Semitic or Sumerian language of Mesopotamia, and we shall probably be not far wrong if we assign to them an antiquity of not less than six thousand years. It will, of course, be understood that the versions which are rendered into English in the following pages do not belong to this early date, but it is more than probable that they represent substantially an extremely ancient recension. Since they were drawn up for the Royal Library at Nineveh by the command of Ashurbanipal about the first half of the seventh century before Christ, we are fully justified in assuming that due care was shown by the court scribes in the choice of their materials.

The various groups of texts translated herein may be briefly described as follows :—

(1) The Ašakki marṣûti, i.e., a Series of tablets which were composed with the view of curing the "Fever-sickness." The number of tablets in the Series was not less than twelve, and the material consisted of exorcisms and spells, which were directed against the disease *Ašakku*. I have here translated this word by "fever," because the symptoms exhibited by a man suffering from the *Ašakku*-disease closely resemble those of one smitten by intermittent fever, or by malaria. It must, however, be remembered that the translation of *Ašakku* by "fever" is tentative.

(2) The Ṭi'i, i.e., a Series of tablets which were composed with the view of curing headache; the number of tablets in the Series consisted of nine, and their contents are charms and incantations which were used to drive away pains of all kinds in the head. In the present state of our knowledge it is impossible to say whether the early Sumerians distinguished between the various forms of headache which are accompanied by nausea, vomiting, etc.

(3) A series of miscellaneous texts containing charms, spells, and incantations, similar in character to that of the texts described in paragraphs (1) and (2). It is perfectly clear that they were written for the purpose of driving diseases of various kinds out of the body, but it is unfortunately impossible in all cases in the present state of our knowledge to say what

those infirmities were. We are, however, certain from the contents of the Tablet which I have called "U," that this document was composed with the express purpose of affording relief to those unfortunate wights who had been so unlucky as to have come under the influence of the Evil Eye.

(4) The next group of tablets is called LUḪ-KA, a title for which the meaning "Cleansing of the Mouth" may be suggested tentatively. Whether this be its exact rendering or not matters comparatively little, but we are certain that the texts were written for the purpose of restoring to ceremonial purity a man who had wittingly or unwittingly become contaminated or impure through touching or even beholding some unclean thing. The compositions of this group were, in short, intended to destroy one of the many forms of *tapu* to which, according to ancient Sumerian tradition, mankind was peculiarly liable.

(5) A group of tablets which contain descriptions of a number of supernatural beings, which corresponded roughly to the modern Arabic *Jinn* and *Jann*. The identification of the greater number of these is difficult; among those worthy of special note is the goddess NIN-TU, who is said to wear an elaborate tiara and veil, and to be girt about the loins with a zone or garment, her breast being uncovered. The upper part of her body is that of a naked woman, and the lower part is said to be scaly like the skin of a snake. It is important

from many points of view to observe that she is represented suckling her babe at the left breast. In the course of the excavations which have been made in Assyria during the last fifty years, numbers of clay figures possessing the characteristics described above have been found, and we are probably right in considering that they are intended to be votive figures of the goddess NIN-TU, which have been offered to her by devout but barren women who desired offspring. (For specimens of these figures see the Babylonian and Assyrian Room in the British Museum, Nos. 91,853-91,854.) There is little doubt that NIN-TU occupied among the peoples of Mesopotamia the position which Hathor held among the Egyptians and the Virgin Mary among Oriental Christian peoples. She was, in fact, a form of the World-Mother, or Chief Mother-Goddess, who plays such an important part in many mythologies.

(6) A text which supplies us with a unique version of the Legend of the Worm, i.e., with a copy of a very ancient prescription for curing the toothache. One of the most interesting characteristics of the legend is the manner in which the genesis of the Worm is traced by a series of steps from Anu, the Sky-god, and we see how even an evil thing may be derived from a divine source. Similarly, we may note the fact that the magician would sometimes assert that the evil which he was about to combat was so powerful that it had at some remote period vanquished even

the gods themselves. Thus, in Col. III of K. 191 we are told that the *šam libbi*, i.e., "Heart-plant," on one occasion overcame the heart of Shamash, the Sun-god, and of Sin, the Moon-god, and that it also had power over the hearts of men and animals; and it is perfectly clear that the "Heart-plant" must have possessed some intoxicating and narcotic effect. We may note in passing that this text states that the plant grew in Matan, which is usually identified with the Sinaitic Peninsula, and I venture to suggest the identification of the *šam libbi* with the *Hyoscyamus muticus*, which I have seen growing in the Peninsula, and the natives told me that this plant possessed highly intoxicating properties, in fact they call it *saykarân*, i.e., that which intoxicates.[1]

One of the most important results obtained from the study of the above-mentioned texts is the discovery of the existence of the *tapu* among the Sumerians and their successors, the Babylonians and Assyrians. It seems that it was almost impossible for man to avoid falling under some *tapu* or ban, and it is clear that the Semitic inhabitants of Western Asia must have derived their knowledge of this remarkable superstition from the earlier non-Semitic inhabitants of the country. With the existence of the *tapu* among the Sumerians I have been acquainted for some time

[1] For the text and a German rendering see Dr. Kuchler's *Beiträge*, Leipzig, 1904, p. 9 ff.

past, but to M. Fossey belongs the credit of being the first to publish an account of it, and to give the texts on which his deductions were based. For his views on the subject the reader is referred to his careful work *La Magie Assyrienne*, which appeared in 1902. Finally, mention must be made of another important discovery of the existence among the Sumerians of ceremonies which prove that this people had developed the idea of the "Atonement" several hundreds of years before the Hebrews. The verb used is *kuppuru*, which, as Dr. Zimmern has pointed out, is identical with the Hebrew word כִּפֶּר.

The ideas and beliefs which actually underlie the Levitical ceremonies of the "Atonement" are still but imperfectly understood, but I believe that the study of the texts in which the "Atonement" of the Sumerians is mentioned and described will do much to indicate the method to be followed in dealing with this important subject.

In conclusion, my thanks are due to Dr. E. A. Wallis Budge and Mr. L. W. King for much help in writing this book.

R. CAMPBELL THOMPSON.

LONDON, January 1st, 1904.

CONTENTS.

SERIES AŠAKKI MARṢÛTI.

SERIES ṬI'I.

MISCELLANEOUS INCANTATIONS.

SERIES LUḪ-KA.

DESCRIPTIONS OF GODS, ETC.

LEGEND OF THE WORM.

Introduction.

Introduction.

In the first volume of this work the texts treated of belonged chiefly to the Series entitled "The Evil Spirits," and dealt with the relations which existed between men and demons, and provided the spells whereby the evil which had attacked a sick man might be removed. The incantations of the two Series "Fever Sickness" and "Headaches" which are translated in the present volume are of a similar character, but the formulæ prescribed must be classed under the head of sympathetic magic to an even greater extent than those of the preceding Series, and the exorcisms go far to show that the *tapu* (more commonly known as *taboo*) was as real a terror to the Assyrians as it was to the other Semitic tribes. The more this class of texts is examined, the more closely are their contents found to resemble the magic of other nations. This is proved by the following considerations:—

(1) Words of Power.

In attacking the powers of evil it was of no avail for the magician to rely solely on his own strength; it was necessary for him to call to his aid some divine authority to support him in his combat. This aid is generally known as the "Word of Power," and in its simplest form is the name of some divine being or thing. It is for this reason that so many of the Assyrian incantations end with the words

> "By Heaven be ye exorcised! By Earth be ye exorcised!"

at which adjuration the evil spirits are supposed to be overcome. It is also common to find long lists of gods invoked in the same way and for the same purpose.

But in addition to this simple form there are many elaborations which can all be traced back to the same fountain-head. For instance, in many exorcisms against diseases which were supposed to be caused by the agency of spirits, we find the sorcerer repeating the legend which tells how Marduk went to Ea, his father, to ask his advice against the sickness which possesses the sick man for whom he is reciting the incantation:—

> "Marduk hath seen him (the sick man) and
> "Unto the house of his father Ea hath entered and spoken:
> "'Father' [1]
> "Twice he hath said unto him,
> "'What this man shall do he knoweth not,
> "'Whereby he may be assuaged.'

[1] Here Marduk repeats the first line of the tablet.

" Ea hath answered his son Marduk :
" 'O my son, what dost thou not know,
" 'What more can I give thee?
" 'O Marduk, what dost thou not know,
" 'How can I add unto thy knowledge?
" 'What I know thou knowest also.
" 'Go, my son Marduk' "[1] ——

Then follow the advice of Ea and his instructions for healing the patient. This legend is constantly repeated in the incantations, and it was so well known that it is generally quoted on the tablets in an abbreviated form in one line in the following way: "Marduk hath seen him: 'What I'; 'Go, my son' "; the priest or magician supplying the remainder and reciting it in full.

Now, it is not difficult to see that the mention of this episode is based on a fundamental principle of all magic, viz., the use of Words of Power, for rites and ceremonies have no inherent authority of their own, and are only of avail when used in conjunction with supernatural aid. By bringing in the story of Ea and Marduk, the magician at once invokes divine help, and, in so far as he carries out the directions which Ea gives to his son, it is as though Marduk were himself performing the incantation, the exorcist becoming the servant of the god, endowed with

[1] See note *d*, p. 117 of Vol. I.

corresponding power against spirits. Indeed, magic, be it worked by spell or amulet, depends largely on these Words of Power written or recited, and a similar use of magical words is to be found among other ancient nations. For instance, we find in the Egyptian Pyramid Texts of Unas (c. 3500 B.C.) that it is stated that "a book with words of magical power" was buried with him.[1] No demon could withstand the authority of these mystic words if only they were rightly employed, particularly if used in the proper place, and with the proper intonation, and by a properly qualified priest.

We have seen, then, that Ea and Marduk, two of the most powerful gods of Assyria, especially in all matters relating to sorcery, were supposed to help magicians, should they be invoked to aid them in their spells. The use of mighty names in exorcisms, and the invocations to the gods to lay the evil under a ban, had each its special significance. The human sorcerer with all his ceremonies and abracadabra was powerless against supernatural evil unless he could depend on the aid of some more powerful spirit, and since the gods were vested with authority over all evil, it was the gods to whom he turned in his hour of need. The system is a universal one, and lies at the base of all magic, whether it be the spells of the Sumerian priest who exorcised a demon two

[1] See Budge, *Egyptian Magic*, p. 28.

or three thousand years before Christ, or a Syrian monk casting out devils, or a mediæval wizard summoning a familiar spirit. The only difference lies in the actual divine word which was used; the Babylonian priest adjures the evil spirit by one of the gods, or by heaven and earth, while the later wizards invoke the name of Christ. Each trusts to the god in whom he believes to lay the devil under a ban.

It is also plain from these texts that the Assyrian sorcerer considers himself in direct communication with the gods, being merely the mouthpiece through which the divine will acts. Indeed, he claims to be sent by the gods when he is expelling a demon:—

"The man of Ea am I!
"The man of Damkina am I!
"The messenger of Marduk am I!
"To revive the ( ) sick man,
"The great lord Ea hath sent me;
"He hath added his pure spell to mine,
"He hath added his pure voice to mine,
"He hath added his pure spittle to mine,
"He hath added his pure prayer to mine."[1]

And at the end of his exorcism he prays to Ea[2]:—

"O Ea, King of the Deep, to see . . .
"I, the magician, am thy slave.

[1] *Devils and Evil Spirits*, Vol. I, Tablet III, l. 65 ff.
[2] Ibid., l. 260.

"March thou on my right hand,
"Be present on my left;
"Add thy pure spell unto mine,
"Add thy pure voice unto mine,
"Vouchsafe (to me) pure words,
"Make fortunate the utterances of my mouth,
"Ordain that my decisions be happy,
"Let me be blessed where'er I tread,
"Let the man whom I (now) touch be blessed.
"Before me may lucky thoughts be spoken,
"After me may a lucky finger be pointed.
"Oh that thou wert my guardian Genius,
"And my guardian Spirit!"

Now the idea that the sorcerer was the direct agent of the divine will continued down to the Middle Ages, when the wizard in uttering his spells describes himself as "the servant of the Most High."[1]

The intention of the magician when combating these evil spirits is to bind them in such a way, with the help of the Mighty Names, that they can do no more harm. In all Assyrian magical texts great stress is laid on the banning or tabooing of the demons by the divine powers which the priest invokes, i.e., either the names of gods or, far more frequently, the powers of heaven and earth. The phrase "By Heaven be ye exorcised! By Earth be ye exorcised!" calls in all

[1] See p. xxx.

celestial and earthly powers against the invisible foes, who will thus be spellbound. In the same way, some thousands of years later in the same country the descendants of these people, the holy Nestorian monks, were credited with the ability to exorcise devils and lay them under a ban in the name of Christ. It is related of Rabban Hormizd, the Persian, that he once overcame certain devils in this way :—

" Straightway the devils of the impure Ignatius [began] to buzz in the air,
" And they took the miserable man up and held him suspended in the air ;
" Suddenly our father fixed a sharp arrow in his bow,
" And shot it at the miserable man and his legions and pierced his heart ;
" He made the deceiving devils to hear [these words] :—' It is not meet for you
" ' To fulfil in him your will with the fulness of impurity :
" ' By Jesus Christ I bind you, O ye trembling horde,
" ' So that ye may abide in the air as ye are in hot agitation,
" ' And ye shall continue to abide in terror until I loose you from the bond.' " [1]

[1] E. A. Wallis Budge, *The Histories of Rabban Hormizd*, p. 474.

(2) Knowledge of the Supernatural Enemy.

Words of power, therefore, plainly constitute one of the first principles of magic. The next principle, and one no less important, consists in the knowledge of the name or characteristics of the unseen influence which afflicts the sick man. It is, however, not necessary that the diagnosis should be exact, for it cannot be expected that a magician should be able to define the exact form of the invisible demon or *tapu* which has assailed his patient. Devils are legion, and *tapus* may arise from countless unknown or forgotten causes, and neither can be distinctly specified ; yet it is absolutely necessary that the spirit or evil influence shall be mentioned by name in order that, by whatsoever power it be that it is removed, there shall be no doubt as to what is meant. To this end, therefore, the priest repeats long lists of ghosts, devils, or *tapus*, any one of which may be the cause of the sickness, and by so doing he impresses the demon that he is in possession of his name or description. The idea underlying this custom is that when once he possesses the name of his enemy he has gained the mastery over some portion of him, and just as he is able to cast spells upon living people if he has some of their nail-parings, or hair, or even wax figures in their likeness, so is he able to conjure the hostile spirit because he knows its name. This is exemplified in the customs of the natives of many savage tribes, who are afraid to disclose their names lest some enemy should hear it and thereby be able to work magic against them.[1] Thus, "an "Australian black is always very unwilling to tell his "real name, and there is no doubt that this reluctance "is due to the fear that through his name he may be "injured by sorcerers."[2] Among the ancient Egyptians the monster Apep could be destroyed by making a wax figure of him, and after writing his name upon it by casting it into the fire;[3] and it is evident that the writing of the name is considered as good as moulding nail-parings into the wax, the difference being that Apep is a demon and nothing tangible can be obtained of him. In Palestinian Demonology the same thing is apparent in the words of the Unclean Spirit (Luke iv, 34), "Art thou come to destroy us? I know "thee who thou art; the Holy One of God."

In the magic of the Middle Ages, if a demon was slow to appear at the command of the wizard, he rendered himself liable to be cursed and buried in oblivion, because his master knew his name and "seal." In one of the Grimoires, or books on magic, the student of sorcery is recommended to write the seal of the demon on a piece of parchment and put it into a box "with brimstone, assafœtida, and other stinking

[1] On this see Frazer, *Golden Bough* (2nd ed.), i, 404.

[2] R. Brough Smith, *Aborigines of Victoria*, i, 469 (quoted ibid.).

[3] Budge, *Egyptian Magic*, p. 171.

perfumes"; he must then exorcise the demon and threaten to destroy him.

"... I, who am the servant of the Most High
"... will excommunicate thee, will destroy thy
"name and seal which I have in this box, will burn
"them with unquenchable fire, and bury them in un-
"ending oblivion ..."[1]

Consequently, when we find long repetitions of the names of ghosts and all the possible forms of death which may have overtaken them when alive on earth, or lists of demons with their peculiar characteristics, it is plain that the magician expects to vanquish the spirit as soon as he shows that he knows its name. It is immaterial that he himself should know exactly which one it is out of the long categories which he reels off; it is only necessary for him to make the list of possible demons sufficiently inclusive to contain the description or name of the particular demon which he wishes to exorcise, and it is enough that he should repeat its name in some form or other, that it should cease from troubling his patient. Indeed, this is the idea of what may be termed the poetical part of the Assyrian spells, which all begin with long descriptions of the particular demon which it is intended to drive out.

[1] Arthur Edward Waite, *The Book of Black Magic*, p. 199.

(3) Ritual and Ceremonies.

There is still a third component to these texts, and this is the ritual and magic symbolism, especially in conjunction with certain stones, plants, hair, animals, etc., without which the ceremony, particularly in sympathetic magic, is incomplete. In the cases where Marduk is supposed to ask his father Ea for advice, the god returns with directions for purely magical ceremonies with loaves of bread, reeds, water, wax figures, and all kinds of objects which had magical powers if properly used. Many of these charms in early use in Mesopotamia are still employed among the modern Semitic descendants, and the methods of using them are just the same as they were three or four thousand years ago.

Animals and their hair were largely used in these ceremonies, and great stress was laid on their being undefiled. A young pig, a virgin kid, or its hair, are frequently mentioned, and this condition of ceremonial purity was imposed on the use of such beasts even as late as the Middle Ages, when the "virgin kid" was largely used by wizards in the making of parchment which was to be inscribed with magical spells.[1] In these incantations it becomes purely a question of sympathetic magic, and the animal, be it pig or kid, when killed, is placed near the body

[1] Waite, *Book of Black Magic*, p. 209.

of the patient as a substitute for him in which the demoniacal influence may be absorbed. Thus it is advised in certain cases of sickness to take a "white kid of the god Tammuz," and, after taking out its heart and giving it to the sufferer to hold, the magician must lay the carcase down close to him and utter various chants over them. The baneful power will then pass from the man into the carcase, which must forthwith be cast forth from the house. This killing of the kid is elaborated in another recipe for the same disease, which tells how Ea gave advice to his son Marduk for the benefit of the sufferer :—

"The kid is the substitute for mankind,
"He hath given the kid for his life,
"He hath given the head of the kid for the head of the man,
"He hath given the neck of the kid for the neck of the man,
"He hath given the breast of the kid for the breast of the man." [1]

That is to say, the body of the kid will receive the sickness which at present annoys the man. A tradition very similar to this is found in Morocco, and a man who has a headache will sometimes take

[1] See Tablet N. This is the text which Professor Sayce quoted as proving that the idea of vicarious punishment was already conceived of, and that the sacrifice of children was a Babylonian institution. *Hibbert Lectures*, p. 78.

a lamb or goat and beat it until it falls down, believing that the headache will thus be transferred to the animal.[1]

Instead of the kid a sucking-pig might be taken, and after its heart had been removed its bristles were to be put on the head of the man, of course symbolical of his hair, its blood sprinkled on the sides of the bed, and the carcase opened and spread out on his limbs.

"Give the pig in his stead,
"And give the flesh as his flesh,
"The blood as his blood,
"And let him take it;
"Its heart (which thou hast set on his heart)
"Give as his heart,
"And let him take it."

Now the most remarkable parallel to this spell is contained in the New Testament story of the Gadarene swine. The devils which possess the two men beseech Jesus Christ, if He cast them out, to send them into the herd of swine which is feeding close at hand, and when the devils leave the men they at once take up their abode in the swine, which, according to the story, go mad and rush down the hill into the water, where they are drowned. Undoubtedly here is some reminiscence of the Assyrian or some similar tradition; in the cuneiform text we find the disease-

[1] Dopper, *Descr. de l'Afrique*, quoted Frazer, *Golden Bough* (1st ed.), ii, p. 169.

devil leaving the possessed man at the sorcerer's invocation and entering the body of the pig. In the New Testament story, the swine are represented as alive when the demons enter them, but as soon as this happens they are immediately made to destroy themselves. If the body of the pig in the Assyrian incantation is to be thrown away or destroyed, as in the cases both of the kid and the vegetables, it is easy to see in this ending a distinct connection between the two. From the Assyrian incantation another and entirely different inference may be drawn, and this is that neither the Sumerians nor the Assyrians considered the pig an unclean animal. As a rule, no good Hebrew or Mohammedan would consent to touch a pig in this way, much less to have its blood sprinkled on his bed, or its heart laid upon him, although even among the Mohammedans swine's flesh is resorted to as a medicine in extremities. Zwemer[1] relates that Arab patients would come to him for a small piece of the flesh (which they suppose all Christians eat) to cure one in desperate straits.

A further development is the ceremony whereby the evil demons are transferred to a pot of water, which is then broken :—

> "The evil Spirit (and) Ghost that appear in the desert,
> "O Pestilence that has touched the man for harm,

[1] *Arabia*, p. 281.

"The Tongue that is banefully fastened on the man,
"May they be broken in pieces like a goblet,[1]
"May they be poured forth like water."[2]

The intention of the magician is that the demons, which have presumably been transferred to the water in the vessel with which he has been working the spell, will be dissipated when the pot is broken and the water poured forth on the ground. There would be no meaning in it otherwise.

To pass on to a different method which the Babylonian sorcerers used, it is curious to see an unusual development of the common wax-figure hocus-pocus. The system of making a magical wax figure of one's enemy in order to bring him into one's power was as common in Mesopotamia as elsewhere, and need not be discussed here, but there is an inverse process which Babylonian doctors used in order to rid their patients of malignant devils. This was by fashioning an image of the sufferer in some plastic material and by properly recited charms, to induce the demon to leave the human body and enter its waxen counterpart. For instance,[3] one tablet directs that a piece of Sea-Clay should be taken and moulded into the likeness of the patient and placed on his loins at night in order that the Plague-god might be

[1] Cf. Ps. xxxi, 12, and Revelation ii, 27.
[2] Tablet "C," l. 156, Vol. I, p. 151.
[3] Tablet "R."

expelled. Further, at dawn, the "atonement for his body" was to be made, the "Incantation of Eridu" to be performed, and the man's face to be turned to the west. The symbolic use of Sea-Clay here is probably due to its connection with Ea, the god of the Ocean, who is so constantly invoked in charms and spells. There is a similar text[1] wherein the magician makes a figure of the man in dough, and after bringing water to the man he pours out the water of the Incantation :—

"Bring forth a censer and a torch ;
"As the water trickleth away from his body,
"So may the pestilence in his body trickle away ;
"Return these waters into a cup and
"Pour them forth in the broad places."

The demon will then depart from the man's body like the water, and will enter the figure.

An interesting parallel to this example of the use of a magical figure with a good object in view is afforded by a Legend of the Virgin Mary which is preserved in Ethiopic. It seems that a certain merchant was shot in the eye by a pirate at sea, and that his friends were unable to pull out the dart; in these straits he begged his friends to take him to the church of the Virgin, who was in the habit of working cures by means of wax figures. The people of the island on which her shrine stood used to make

[1] Tablet "T."

models of their wounded friends, with representations of the wounds on them, and take them to her, and when offerings had been made by those who brought them, both for the poor and for the church, the Virgin Mary caused the marks of the wounds to disappear from the wax figures, and as they went the men whom the figures represented were made whole. This being so, the friends of the merchant made a wax figure of him, with a dart sticking in one of its eyes, and when they had taken it to the church of the Virgin, and had made suitable gifts to the shrine, Mary had compassion upon the man and pulled the dart out of the eye of the wax figure, and as soon as she had done this the dart fell out of the merchant's eye and he was healed at once.[1]

The tying and loosing of magical knots, symbolic of spells bound or loosed from a person, was a form of magic as common in Assyria as it was and still is in other lands. By tying knots and at the same time chanting some magic words a wizard or witch could cast a *tapu* on an enemy, as is clear from the *Maḳlu* tablet, which ends one incantation against such malevolent beings with these words :—

> " Her knot is loosed, her sorcery is brought to nought,
> " And all her charms fill the desert." [2]

[1] See Budge, *The Miracles of the Blessed Virgin Mary and the Life of Ḥanna (Saint Anne)*, etc., London, 1900, pp. 48–49.

[2] *W.A.I.*, iv, 49, 34*a*.

In driving away a headache the following spell was used by the priest :—

" Take the hair of a virgin kid,
" Let a wise woman spin (it) on the right side
" And double it on the left,
" Bind twice seven knots
" And perform the Incantation of Eridu,
" And bind the head of the sick man,
" And bind the neck of the sick man,
" And bind his life,[1]
" And bind up his limbs ;
" And surround[2] his couch,
" And cast the water of the Incantation over him,
" That the Headache may ascend to heaven
" Like the smoke of a peaceful homestead,
" That like the lees of water poured out
" It may go down into the earth."[3]

A further use of the cord in headache cures is found in the same tablet.[4] Unfortunately the beginning is lost, but at the end directions are given for spinning a threefold cord and tying twice seven knots in it, and after performing the Incantation of Eridu this is to be tied on the head of the sick man. The headache will then go.

[1] Or "soul."
[2] Or "stand round."
[3] See Tablet IX, l. 74.
[4] Ibid., l. 233.

O'Donovan tells the story of a curiously similar method among the modern Persians for removing fever. A woman whose daughter was sick of a fever came to him with a handful of camel's hair that he might make it into a charm for her. He himself, being ignorant of the method by which this should be done, handed it over to a Khan who was with him. "By means of a spindle the camel hair was spun "to a stout thread, the Khan all the time droning "some verses from the Koran or some necromantic "chant. When the thread was finished it was of "considerable length, and folding it three times upon "itself he respun it. Then he proceeded to tie seven "knots upon the string. Before drawing each knot "hard he blew upon it. This, tied in the form of "a bracelet, was to be worn on the wrist of the "patient. Each day one of the knots was to be "untied and blown upon, and when the seventh knot "had been undone the whole of the thread was to be "made into a ball and thrown into the river, carrying, "as was supposed, the illness with it." [1]

(4) Tapu.[2]

In primitive communities certain social restrictions arise from the fear of the supernatural, that is to say,

---

[1] *Merv Oasis*, ii, 319.

[2] On this subject see M. Fossey's chapter in his *La Magie Assyrienne* (1902), p. 52.

a ban or *tapu* is laid on certain elements which from their nature are either holy or unclean. The totem of a tribe from its nature is *tapu*, and, if it be an animal, its flesh is prohibited as food to the members of that tribe; if a man has rendered himself unclean by his actions or condition he is set apart from the rest of his fellows lest he should communicate his dangerous state to the others, and so bring down the divine anger upon them as well. To the primitive man certain natural states or functions are dangerous from the fear of something supernatural, and all who are affected by them are temporarily placed under a ban.

In the Babylonian legends of the relations between gods and men, instances of anything which might be referred to the idea of *tapu* are not common. Possibly we may see this influence in one of the incidents related in the Gilgamish Epic.[1] The goddess Ishtar, enraged at the refusal of her advances by the hero Gilgamish, creates a divine bull to destroy him, but he and his comrade Ea-bani slay it after a fierce encounter. At this Ishtar utters a curse against these two who have dared thus to challenge her power, and probably as a consequence Ea-bani dies and Gilgamish is smitten with a sore sickness. Here the goddess does not curse them until they have killed the divine bull, and the fundamental idea is

[1] See King, *Babylonian Religion*, p. 161.

therefore very much the same as that of many *tapus* concerning holy things. But there are many circumstances connected with this incident which it is impossible in our present state of knowledge to explain adequately, and it must therefore be understood that the suggested explanation is merely tentative.

In the magical texts, on the other hand, the principle of the ban and *tapu* underlies everything, both the affection of the sick man and the method of exorcising the devil which possesses him. For demons as well as mankind are subject to the divine *tapu*, and it is on this principle that the magic of the incantations depends, since the priest invokes the help of the gods to drive away the evil spirit, and to lay it under a ban and bind it. In the Assyrian exorcisms, when the prayers end with the line

> " By Heaven be thou exorcised! By Earth be thou exorcised!"

it is intended that the powers of Heaven and Earth shall lay the demon under a *tapu*.

The divine *tapu* against spirits is described in one of the exorcisms in the following words :—

> " Ban! Ban! *Tapu*[1] that none can pass,
> " *Tapu* of the gods that none may break,
> " *Tapu* of heaven and earth that none can change,

---

[1] The word used here is *uṣurtu*, which is derived from a root akin to the Hebrew עָצַר.

"Which no god may annul,
"Nor god nor man can loose,
"A snare without escape, set for evil,
"A net whence none can issue forth, spread for evil."[1]

This principle of banning evil spirits is common to all systems of magic.

The influence of the *tapu* on human beings as a consequence of certain deeds or conditions was as prevalent among the Assyrians and Babylonians as among other primitive tribes. A great part of the series *Shurpu* is devoted to the removal of the *mamit* ("ban" or "*tapu*") which the man has wittingly or unwittingly incurred, and this *mamit* falls into classes, the one incurred by what at first sight appear to be breaches of ordinary social morality, such as murder, adultery, and theft,[2] and the second by distinct ceremonial uncleanness, such as touching the bed or chair of a person under a *tapu*,[3] or through the hostility of some enemy who has the power of bewitching him. There is no doubt that the *tapu* of uncleanness was as widely recognized among the Babylonians as among other nations; indeed, one incantation is entirely given up to the methods of purifying a certain person[4] who has in some way become unclean either from

[1] See Tablet "V," l. 1.
[2] *Shurpu*, Tablet II, 47 ff.
[3] Ibid., 100 ff.
[4] In this case it is the *mašmašu*, or magician, who is to be cleansed.

touching dirty water or even merely casting his eye upon someone unclean :—

"While he walked in the street,
". . . while he walked in the street,
"While he made his way through the broad places,
"While he walked along the streets and ways,
"He trod in some libation that had been poured forth, or
"He put his foot in some unclean water,
"Or cast his eye on the water of unwashen hands,
"Or came in contact with a woman of unclean hands,
"Or glanced at a maid with unwashen hands,
"Or his hand touched a bewitched woman,
"Or he came in contact with a man of unclean hands,
"Or saw one with unwashen hands,
"Or his hand touched one of unclean body."[1]

Marduk then repeats this to Ea and asks how the man shall be purified, and in the ceremony which follows, sacred lavers play a large part. Here we undoubtedly have a most elementary form of ban; the man has become *tapu* because he has inadvertently come into contact with something or someone unclean. According to the explanatory text K. 156 (l. 68 ff.),[2] a man might be contaminated by the lees of water which were thrown away undrunk, or by spittle

[1] See Series LUḪ-KA, p. 137.
[2] Haupt, *Akkad. u. Sumer. Keilschr.*, No. 11

"which the dust covereth not"; at least, this is what is to be assumed from the exorcism which is to be recited in order to expel the evil resulting from some connection with them. Again, as was mentioned above, if a man ran up against another who was under a *tapu*, slept on his bed, sat on his chair, ate out of his plate, or drank from his cup, he was liable to the action of *tapu*, and it was necessary to remove such a ban with the help of the priest.[1] Naturally, however, the particular *tapu* which had affected the man was not easily discovered, and it behoved the exorcist who drove away the divine curse which afflicted his patient to include in his chant long categories of possible eventualities, just as he did in expelling demoniac influences. The third tablet of the *Shurpu* series is entirely devoted to this, and gives a list of one hundred and sixty-three *tapus*. It begins in the following way:—

"Marduk, the priest of the gods, can loose
"The *tapu* of every sort which seizeth on
"The man, the son of his god."

And the lines which follow are all on one model—

"He looseth the ban of father or mother which hath seized on the man,
"He looseth the ban of a grandfather, the ban of a grandmother,
"He looseth the ban of brother or sister."

[1] Zimmern, *Shurpu*, Tablet ii, l. 99.

The *tapus* include those which come from the family, old or young, friend or neighbour, rich or poor; oven, bellows, pots and cups, bed or couch, chariot or weapons. To drink out of an unclean vessel, to sit in the sun, to root up plants in the desert, to cut reeds in a thicket, to slay the young of beasts, to pray with unclean hands, and a host of other common actions, might under certain conditions bring a *tapu* on the man.

Now it is plain that if dangerous results were not supposed to ensue on unclean acts there would be no point in banning them. Again, it is absurd to suppose that all this lengthy list of *tapus* in the Shurpu tablet was for the benefit of such as had omitted to wash their hands or vessels on all occasions, unless they gave some physical evidence that they were suffering from the effects of some supernatural hostility. Indeed, the 5th and 6th tablets of *Shurpu* begin with the words, "An evil curse hath fallen on the man like a devil," and the frequently recurring story of Marduk asking Ea for advice is repeated, Ea advising him as follows:—

"Go, O my son Marduk,
"Take him to a holy house of cleansing,
"Release his *tapu*, free his *tapu*!
"The perturbing evil in his body,
"Be it the curse of his father,
"Or the curse of his mother,
"Or the curse of his elder brother,
"Or the curse of some wicked woman
"Whom the man knoweth not."

It is therefore evident that, in early times at least, if a Babylonian fell sick he might be considered *tapu*, such an infliction arising out of his own agency or that of others. So that if a man were attacked by sickness it might be either ascribed to divine punishment for his acts against the gods, to the attacks of spirits, or to a closely allied theme, the curses or spells of some enemy, and for any of these cases he naturally became *tapu* until the spell or ban was lifted from him. This was effected through the aid of a priest, who was able by his knowledge of magical words, prayers, and ceremonies to invoke the gods to help him. By the help of what is known as "sympathetic magic" he was able to transfer the disease to something animate or inanimate, this being described in many cases as "making an atonement" for him, the word in Assyrian being *kuppuru*, exactly the equivalent of the Hebrew *kipper* of the Priestly Code, as was pointed out by Zimmern.[1]

To return to the *tapu* among the Babylonians. We have seen that in this respect they are, as was to be expected, very similar to other nations, but in several things they show what may be an earlier conception of certain of the *tapus*, especially those concerning animals. For instance, the flesh of the

[1] *Ritualtafeln*, p. 92. As he points out, the word in a technical sense was probably borrowed from the Babylonians by the Hebrews, and cannot be referred to a primitive common stock.

pig was *tapu* only on certain days, and not at all times as among the later Hebrews and Mohammedans. In one of the "hemerology" texts these days are specified :—

"If a man eats swine's flesh on the thirtieth of Ab,[1] boils will break out upon him.

"If a man eats the flesh of swine or oxen on the twenty-seventh of Tisri (such and such things will happen to him)."[2]

Originally there seems to be no doubt that animals were sacred from their holy nature, and not from any "uncleanness."[3] The dog, again, although the pariahs may have been held in a natural contempt, does not seem to have held any place among the "unclean" animals, judging from the personal names Kalbâ, Kalbi ("my dog"). It is, however, true that it is not uncommon for scribes in writing to the king to describe themselves as "dogs,"[4] but this may be ascribed to their wish to call attention to their loyalty and fidelity, and not necessarily that they are base serfs. Fish, again, were *tapu* on the ninth of Iyyar,

---

[1] July–August. It must be admitted that this is an obvious sanitary regulation. Compare also the views which the Egyptians held about the pig in chapter cxii of the *Book of the Dead* (ed. Budge, p. 176).

[2] *W.A.I.*, v, 48–49.

[3] See Robertson Smith, *Religion of the Semites*, p. 153.

[4] The people of Kisik do so (Harper, *Assyrian Letters*, No. 210, rev. 8).

under pain of sickness; in Syria, where fish were sacred to Atargatis, if a man ate of them he was liable to be visited by a sickness of ulcers, swellings, or wasting disease.[1] Even dates eaten on a forbidden day might produce ophthalmia. It must be admitted, however, that the element of hygiene probably enters largely into these restrictions, and that in many cases *tapu* has nothing to do with them at all.

Certain days were *tapu* for uttering a ban; "On the nineteenth of Iyyar he who utters a ban—a god will seize upon him."[2] If a man hire a slave on the sixth of Siwan he will not be pleased with him, or if he marry on the twenty-fifth of Iyyar it will turn out unlucky. Sickness will befall the man who crosses a river on the twentieth of Ab.

We find among the Assyrians traces of the Royal *Tapu*, that is to say, the abstention by the king from certain acts. These, however, are only *tapu* to him on the seventh, fourteenth, nineteenth, twenty-first, and twenty-eighth day of the month, that is to say, every seventh day and the forty-ninth (seven × seven) day from the first of the preceding month. These acts are detailed in the "hemerology" tablets, and we may take a specimen.[3]

"The seventh day [of the second Elul] is the "festival day of Marduk and Sarpanitum. A

[1] See Robertson Smith, *Religion of the Semites*, p. 449.

[2] For the Assyrian, see *W.A.I.*, v, pl. 48.

[3] *W.A.I.*, iv, 32; i, 28.

"happy (?) day. An evil day. The shepherd of the "wide-spreading peoples must not eat flesh that has "been cooked over coals, nor bread (cooked) in ashes. "He must not change the clothes of his body, nor "put on white garments. He must not offer sacrifices. "The King must not ride out in his chariot, and must "not raise his voice in command. The priest must "not utter decisions in a secret place. The physician "must not lay his hand on the sick. It is unfitted "for making a curse. In the evening the King should "make offerings and offer sacrifices to Marduk and "Ishtar; his prayer will be pleasing unto the god."

One important point to notice in this hemerology, before going further into the matter of Royal *tapus*, is the distinction drawn between the king and some person who is called "the shepherd of the wide-spreading peoples." If this last is merely an equivalent for "king," as seems quite probable, it is not unlikely that we have here a text that is a recension based upon two different versions.

In these Royal and Priestly *tapus*[1] are the relics of ancient days when priest-kings were accredited with a divine or supernatural nature. The prosperity of the king will result in a like happiness for the nation, and these seventh days or "sabbaths" being evil days, it was not fitting that the ruler of the people

[1] For a full account of the Royal *tapu* among other nations, see Frazer, *Golden Bough* (1900), vol. i, p. 233.

D

should render himself liable to any ban. When the Hebrews borrowed their Sabbath from Babylonia, they altered the conception of it and wove their own myths into the idea until it lost its original significance.

From the instances quoted above, it seems quite plain that *tapu* was a recognized idea among the dwellers in Mesopotamia, and doubtless as the texts are more and more examined the examples will be multiplied.

(5) The Atonement.

From the various passages from the cuneiform texts quoted above it will be seen that the Assyrians were in the habit of performing some ceremony akin to the "Atonement" of the Hebrews. The most striking coincidence, at first sight, is the parallel use of the words *kuppuru* and כִּפֶּר, as has been already noted. In the distinctively priestly phraseology (Ezekiel and "P") the subject of כִּפֶּר is the priest or sometimes the offering[1]; in the cuneiform texts, as far as it is at present known, the verb *kuppuru* is used in incantations only, also with the priest as subject.[2] As these Sumerian incantations are undoubtedly older than the Priestly Code of the Hebrews in its present form, the most probable, if not the only possible, assumption is that the Hebrews took over the

[1] Driver, *Deuteronomy*, p. 426; and see also Robertson Smith, *Old Testament in the Jewish Church*, p. 438.

[2] See Delitzsch, *H.W.B.*, *sub voce*.

Babylonian idea during the Captivity, which thus left its mark on certain of their religious observances.

Now in the following cases of the Hebrew laws, for which an "atonement" is presented, it seems reasonably clear that the idea of *tapu*, just as in modern savage tribes, underlies the whole of them, and that this *tapu* will be removed by the priest's action :—

(1) A woman after childbirth (Lev. xii, 2 ff.).

(2) A person touching anything unclean (Lev. v, 2 ff.).

(3) A man or woman with an issue, or similar uncleanness (Lev. xv, 2 ff.).

(4) A Nazarite defiled by touching a dead body (Numb. vi).

(5) Leprosy, and the house wherein leprosy breaks out (Numb. xiv, 18, 53).

In the Assyrian exorcisms it is plain that the idea of the atonement is the same; the man has incurred some *tapu*, and the priest must remove it by some ceremony which is described by the word *kuppuru*. Consequently we may define the "atonement" as the means by which the supernatural danger which threatens the person lying under the *tapu* is removed from him, and thereby allows him to return to his place in society.

So much for the origin of the ceremony. With regard to the actual ceremonies themselves, there is no doubt that the principle of sympathetic magic is at the base of them. In the Assyrian cases this is at once obvious. For instance, in a certain disease of the head the priest is to lay a white kid of Tammuz alongside the sick man, take out its heart and put it in his hand, and the kid is therefore the material with which an "atonement" is to be made for the man, and it is afterwards to be thrown away.[1] For a similar complaint a headdress (?) is to be made of a clean reed, and after the Incantation of Eridu the priest "makes the atonement" therewith, breaking it over the patient symbolically that it may be a substitute for him.[2] In the case of a certain sickness an image of the patient is made of clay and placed on his loins at night, the "atonement" being made at dawn, or in another case a pot is to be filled with water and various vegetables, and after sprinkling the patient the "atonement" is to be made for him by the priest.[3]

Two of the Hebrew cases give the distinct impression that the origin of the Hebrew "atonement" is to be sought in sympathetic magic. The first one is contained in the directions for cleansing the house in which leprosy appears,[4] where the priest is to take two birds, cedar, scarlet, and hyssop, and after killing one of the birds in an earthen vessel over running water, he is to dip the remainder in the blood of the dead bird and in running water, and to sprinkle the

[1] See Tablet XI, p. 33.
[2] Ibid., Tablet VIII, p. 57.
[3] Ibid., Tablet "R," p. 99.
[4] Lev. xiv, 49.

house seven times; but he shall let go the living bird out of the city into the open fields. The second is the case of the scapegoat on whose head Aaron was to lay the sins of the children of Israel, and send him away by the hand of a "fit man" into the desert to bear their iniquities.[1] Now there is no doubt as to the original signification of this, for the cases are entirely analogous to many of the sympathetic charms which have been already described.

There does not seem to have been any such ceremony as that of the living "Scapegoat" among the Assyrians. M. Fossey (*La Magie Assyrienne*, p. 85) satisfactorily refutes Mr. Prince's theory, which he put forward in the Journal of the American Oriental Society (1900, xxi, pp. 1–22), basing it on the Sumerian text published by Haupt (*Akkad. u. Sumer. Keilschrifttexte*, p. 105). Since then, however, Mr. Prince has put forward another article (*Journal Asiatique*, July–August, 1903, p. 133) maintaining his previous proposition from the same text, which he translates as follows:—"Prends le bouquetin qui allège la douleur; place sa tête sur la tête du malade; du côté du roi, fils de son dieu (c'est-à-dire le patient), chasse-le; que sa salive dans sa bouche coule librement (soit lâchée); que le roi soit pur; qu'il soit sain." M. Fossey has answered it in footnotes to the same paper, and, as he properly points out, "chasse-le" is not the right

[1] Lev. xvi, 21.

translation for U-ME-TE-GUR-GUR, which should be rendered by the Assyrian equivalent *kuppir*, "make the atonement for." Consequently there is nothing to show that the goat was alive, and from a comparison of similar texts in which the animal has obviously been sacrificed (see pp. 17, 29, etc.) it is plain that M. Fossey is correct when he says that the goat was killed (*La Magie Assyrienne*, p. 86).

We may briefly recapitulate, therefore, the important points which the Assyrian magical texts seem to indicate. First, the threefold method of the magician which demanded the "Word of Power" by the invocation of some divine power, the ostentatious knowledge concerning the hostile demon, and the correct use of spells and prescriptions. Secondly, that underneath all the paraphernalia of ritual and ceremonies lies the root-idea of the *tapu*, which will probably be found to be of still greater importance as new material is published. Lastly, the existence of an "atonement" ceremony in Assyria which so curiously parallels certain parts of the Levitical Law, even down to the use of the same word to express this idea. In this last case, as in many others, everything at present points to the Jewish ceremony, as we should expect, having been borrowed from Babylonia. With every new publication of magical texts it becomes plainer how the natives of Chaldea left behind them a reputation for all forms of magic and sorcery, and how greatly they influenced the beliefs of their successors.

Transliterations

and

Translations.

Series Ašakki Marṣûti.

The Third Tablet.

(PLATE I.)

. . . .

UZU . . . .

GAR SAG-GA-NA U-ME . . . .

GAR SU-A-NA U-ME-TE-SU-UB-SU-UB : *a-ka-la* . . . .

ŠU-* UR-* UR-RU-DA-NI E-SIR-KA-* TATTAB-MA-KU U-ME . . . .

tak-pir-ta-šu a-na su-uḳ ir-bit-ti . . . . .

GAR-SAG-IL-LA-NI PU-SAG KALAM-MA-KU U-NE . . . .

pu-uḫ-šu a-na kur-pi ša ma-a-ti iz-ba-am-[*ma*]

A NAM-ŠIB-BA EGIR-BI U-ME-NI-SU : *me-e šip-ti ar-ki-iš zi-ri-i*[*ḳ-ma*]

ZID DINGIR-ŠE-TIR AZAG-GA KA-DINGIR-AŠ-A-AN U-ME-NI . . .

ḳi-im aš-na-an elliti(*ti*) *bâba ka-ma-a pi-rik-*[*ma*]

---

[a] Of Tablet I of this series only the remains of the colophon and the first line of Tablet II ("Incantation:—The evil Spirit sick Fever . . . .") are at present known. (See Plate II.)

[b] *Puḫu.* From the parallelism of S. 747, r. 4 (Martin, *Textes Religieux*, p. 20), "May Ea *puhûa ša ukinnu* . . . my *puḫu*

Series "Fever Sickness."

The Third Tablet.

(PLATE I.)[a]

. . . .

"Flesh . . . .

"[Set] food at his head,

"Satisfy his body with food ;

"[Cast] his 'atonement' to the crossways,

"Leave his 'substitute'[b] to the dungheaps (?) of the land,

"Sprinkle the water of the incantation after it,[c]

"Block up the closed door with pure wheaten flour,

---

which hath been prepared . . . May Marduk *dinanûa ša ibbanû li-šam-g[ir ?]* (thus, and not *li-pa-[aš-šir]*) accept (?) my *dinanû* which hath been made." The preceding lines refer to the *mamît* or "ban" which has fallen upon the man. From Tablet "N," col. iii, ll. 45–46 (*uriṣu dinanû ša ameluti*, "the kid is the substitute for mankind"), it is evident that *dinanû* has the meaning of "substitute" here also, and if so, its parallel *puḫu* will have a similar meaning, which will exactly fit the context above.

[c] Or "afterwards."

[Ḫ]UL-IK IGI-BI BA-RA-AN-DA-NIGIN : *lim-nu pa-ni-šú la u-saḫ-ḫa-[ru-ma]*

[GIG-BAR-A-AN ?] E ŠIG-GA-RA A-BA : *ina mu-ši ma-ši-il bîti ina šu-ḳa-mu-[mi . . .]*

. . . . GAR-NI-DE-A BUR-TA U-ME-NI-LU : *ka-ma-na mi-ri-is šam-ni mu-ru-us-[ma]*

GAR-NI-DE-A BIL-LAL U-ME-NI-LU : *mi-ri-is ṭa-ba-a-ti mu-ru-[us-ma]*

SILA-A-KU U-ME . . . [:] *ana su-ki šu-[kun* (?)*-ma]*

UB - DA - * TATTAB - BA - KU U - ME - [NI - SUM (?)]
ina tu - bu - ḳat ir - bit - ti i - [di (?) *- ma]*

UB E - A - GE DA E - A - GE . . . .
ina tu - bu - ḳat bîti ša - ḫat bîti . . . . .

[GIŠ]-GAL E-A-GE GIŠ-ŠAGIL E-A-GE GIŠ-SAK-KUL . . . .
da-lat bi-ti me-dil bi-ti [sik-kur bi-ti] . . . .

ZI DINGIR - GAL - GAL - E - NE - GE [U - ME - NI - PA]
niš ilâni[pl] *rabûti*[pl] *[tum - me - ma]*

UTUG-ḪUL A-LA-ḪUL GIDIM-ḪUL MUL[LA-ḪUL DINGIR-ḪUL MAŠKIM-ḪUL]
LIL - LA SIR - SIR - E - NE KAN . . . . .
u-tuk-ku lim-nu a-lu-u lim-nu e-[kim-mu lim-nu gal-lu-u lim-nu ilu lim-nu]
ra-bi-ṣu lim-nu šu-nu zi-ḳi-ḳu [mut-taš-rab-bi-ṭu . . . .]

" (That) nothing evil may turn its face (hither and)

" When [he] waketh in the house at midnight

" Mash up a bread-cake[a] with a mash of oil,

" Mash up a mash of wine,

" Put it (?) in the street and

" Place it at the Four Points and

" In the precincts of the house, the vicinity of the house . . . .

" The house-door, the bolt of the house, [the bar of the house] . . . .

" [Invoke] the Great Gods

" That the evil Spirit, the evil Demon, the evil Ghost,
" [The evil Devil, the evil God], the evil Fiend,
" The roaming windblast . . . .

[a] On *kamanu* see Jensen, *Mythen und Epen* (K.B. VI), p. 511, and Zimmern, *Babylonische Religion* (*Ritualtafeln*), p. 144, note 2. On *mirsu* see Zimmern, ibid., p. 99.

[NAM (?)] - TAR - ḪUL - A SU - A - NA GAL . . . .
[*nam-tar* (?)] *lim-nu ša ina zu*-[*um-ri-šu ba-šu-u*]

. . . . DINGIR (?) . . . .
. . . *amelu ša a* . . . .

MULU-GIŠGAL-LU-BI DINGIR-EN-KI DINGIR-[ID ḪE-I-I]
amelu šu-u *ilu* *E - a* *ilu* *Id* [*lit* (?)] - *ta* - ' - [*id*]

I DINGIR - EN - KI - GE PA - ḪE - E - A - [GE]
a - mat *ilu* *E - a* *liš - te - p*[*i*]

DINGIR - DAM - GAL - NUN - NA ḪE - EN - SI - DI - [E]
ilu *Dam - ki - na* *liš - te - šir*

DINGIR - SILIG - ELIM - NUN - NA DU - SAG ZU - AB - GE
* ŠAG - GA TAG - TAG - LI - BI ZA - [A - KAN]
ilu *Marduk mâru riš-tu-u ša ap-si-i bu-un-nu-u*
du-um-mu-ḳu ku-[*um-ma*]

INIM-INIM-MA SIGIŠŠE-SIGIŠŠE GAB-RI SAḪ-TUR-RA

EN UTUG - ḪUL E - SIR - RA GIL - GIL . . . .
Duppi III *KAM* EN AZAG - GIG - [GA - MEŠ]
[*E*]*kal* *m ilu* *Aššur-bani-apli šar kiš*-[*ša*]-*ti šarru* . . . .

[Etc.]

" The evil Plague (?) which [resteth on] his body

" . . . the man . . . . [they may remove and]

" Let that man [glorify] Ea (and) Id,

" May the Word of Ea make clear,

" May Damkina guide aright ;

" O Marduk ! Eldest son of the Deep,
" Thine is the power to brighten and bless ! "[a]

PRAYER FOR SACRIFICING THE SUBSTITUTED (?) SUCKING-PIG.

Incantation :—" The evil Spirit destroyeth in the street."

THIRD TABLET OF THE SERIES " FEVER SICKNESS."

[a] From a comparison of similar texts, it is evident that this is the advice which Ea gives to his son Marduk.

Tablet "L."

REVERSE.

(PLATE II.)

. . . .

. . . -*pal bîti e ta-* . . . .

UTUG-ḪUL BAR-KU ḪE-IM-[TA-GUB]

A-LA-ḪUL BAR-KU [„]

ALAD-ḪUL BAR-KU [„]

GIDIM-ḪUL BAR-KU [„]

MULLA-ḪUL BAR-KU [„]

DINGIR-UTUG-*ŠIG-GA ḪE-EN-DA-LAḪ-[LAḪ-GI-EŠ]

LAMMA-*ŠIG-GA ḪE- [„]

ALAD-*ŠIG-GA ḪE- [„]

KAGAR-*ŠIG-GA ḪE- [„]

MULU-GIŠGAL-BI ḪE-EN-AZAG ḪE-EN-EL ḪE-EN-LAḪ-[LAḪ-GA]

ŠU-*ŠAG-GA DINGIR-RA-NA-KU MULU-GIŠGAL-BI GE . . . .

INIM-INIM-MA SIGIŠŠE-SIGIŠŠE GAB-RI SAḪ-TUR-RA . . .

EN UTUG-ḪUL SILA LIL-LA SIG-GA . . . . .

EN AZAG-GIG-GA SU MULU KA-MU-UN . . . . [*duppi* . .] KAM-ME EN AZAG-GIG-GA

Ekal [m] *Aššur-bani-apli šar kiššati šar* [mâtu] *Aššuri* [KI]

[Etc.]

Tablet "L."

REVERSE.

(PLATE II.)[a]

. . . .

May the evil Spirit [stand] aside,
May the evil Demon [stand] aside,
May the evil Genius [stand] aside,
May the evil Ghost [stand] aside,
May the evil Devil [stand] aside;
May a kindly Spirit be present,
May a kindly Genius be present,
May a kindly Guardian be present,
May a kindly Thought be present,
That this man may become pure, become clean, become bright!
Into the favouring hands of his god may this man [be commended!].

PRAYER FOR SACRIFICING THE SUBSTITUTED (?) SUCKING-PIG . . .

Incantation:—"The evil Spirit which in the street creates a storm wind . . . . . ."
Incantation:—"The evil Fever the body of the man . . . . ."

—TH TABLET OF THE SERIES "FEVER SICKNESS."

---

[a] All that is at present known of Tablet IX is published on Plate II. It apparently ended very much in the same way as Tablet "L," and it gives the beginning of the Tenth Tablet of the Series as "Incantation:—Fever destructive . . ."

Tablet "M."

(PLATE III.)

21. EN AZAG-ḪUL-IK : *a-šak-ku lim-nu ki*[1] *a-bu-bu*[2] *te-bi-ma* : A-MA-TU-GIM ZI-[GA]

IM-GAL KU-KU : *nam-ri-ir-ri la-biš irṣitim(tim) ra-pa-aš-ti*[3] *ma-la* : KUR-DAGAL-LA-A . . .

[ME]LAM DUL-LA : *me-lam-mu*[4] *ka-tim ra-šub-ba-ti*[5] *ra-mi* : IM-ḪUŠ RI-A (?)

[E]-SIR-RA GIN : *suḳi*[6] *it-ta-na-al-lak ina su-ul-la-a*[7] *it-ta-na-at-bak* : E-SIR-RA ŠU-[ŠU]

25. . . . GUB-BA : *i-di a-me-lu iz-za-az-zu man-ma ul ip-[pal-la]-as-su* : MULU IGI . . .

. . . . . : *i-di a-me-lu uš-[ša]-ba-ma man-ma ul* . . . *-su* : MULU NA . . .

. . . . :] *ana bîti ina e-[ri]-bi-šu it-ta-šu ul [u]-ta-ad-du* : ŠI . . . .

. . . . *ina a-ṣi-šu ul iḫ-ḫa-as-[sa]-as* : IZ-KU-PI . . . .

. . . . . *in-na-as-saḫ* " " *iš-šak-kan* : A . . . .

30. . . . . . . TA . . A-NI-KU MULU NA ME (?) . . .

. . . . *man - ma ul* . . . .

. . . . IM - MI - IN . . . .

. . . . *im* (?) . . *ri u ša* . . . .

. . . .

Tablet "M."

(Plate III.)

Incantation :—

The evil Fever hath come like a deluge, and
Girt with dread brilliance it filleth the broad earth,
Enveloped in terror it casteth fear abroad ;
It roameth through the street, it is let loose in the road ;
It standeth beside a man, yet none can see it,
It sitteth beside a man, yet none can [see it].
When it entereth the house its appearance is unknown,
When it goeth forth [from the house] it is not perceived,
. . . . . is removed ,, ,, is set
. . . . none [knoweth ?]
. . . .

[1–7] From K. 4,663.

[1] Adds *ma*. [2] *bi*.

[3] *irṣitu(tu) rapaštu(tu)* for *irṣitim(tim) ra-pa-aš-ti*.

[4] *me*. [5] *tum*.

[6] *su-ḳi*. [7] *su-li-e* (?) for *su-ul-la-a*.

Tablet "N."

Obverse.

Col. I (Plate IV).

. . . . TA KALAM - MA - TA BA - RA - E
[KALAM (?)] KALAM-MA ANA-TA KI-TA LU-LU
[e-kim ?]-mu la ṭa-a-bu ana ma-a-ti u-ṣa-am-ma
ni - iš mâti e - liš u šap - liš id - luḫ
DINGIR-LUGAL NAM-EN-NA DUGUD-DA KUR-RA
LA BA - AN - GAR U - ŠU - UŠ - TA GAR - GAR - RA
be - en - nu mi - iḳ - tu ša ana ma - a - ti
la i - nu - uḫ - ḫu da - um - ma - tu i - šak - ka - nu
ALAD UTUG MAŠKIM GAL-GAL-LA NAM-MULU-GIŠGAL-LU
SILA - DAGAL - LA AL - KAS - KAS - NE - NE
še-e-du u-tuk-ku ra-bi-ṣu rab-bu-ti ša ana niši^{pl}
ri - ba - a - ti it - ta - na - aš - rab - bi - ṭu
U - ḪUŠ GAL UD . . . . GAB - BI
NU-UN . . . . [EGIR-BI IGI-MU]-UN-BAR-RA
ûmu izzu gal-lu-tu . . . i (?)-da (?)-gil i-rat-su
la ut - tar - ru ana arki - šu la ip - pal - [la - as]
DINGIR-UGUR NAM-EN-NA E-SIR-[RA (?)] . . . .
. . . . GIM AZAG (?) - GA . . . .
. . . .

[Remainder of the column lost.]

Col. II.

. . . .
ŠU - AZAG - GA . . . .
a - na ḳa - ti [elliti] . . . .
* GIR UDUN EL . . . .
ana ki - i - ri u u - [tu] - un . . . .

Tablet "N."

Obverse.

Col. I (Plate IV).[a]

An evil ghost (?) hath assailed the land,
And perturbeth the people of the land above and below :
5. A pestilence, a plague that giveth the land no rest,
Hath cast a desolation upon it ;
10. The great Demon, Spirit, and Fiend,
Which roam the broad places for men,
15. The angry, quaking storm [which if one] seeth,
He turneth not nor looketh back again.
A pestilence in the street Nergal [hath brought]

. . . .

Col. II.

. . . .

Upon clean hands . . . .
5. On pitch (?)[b] and coalpan . . . . . .

---

[a] It is not known to which Series this tablet belongs.

[b] *Kîru* is variously translated as "outer wall" or "pitch" (see Muss-Arnolt, *Dictionary*, *sub voce*).

GAR - NAM GAR - GAL - LA KALAM ḪI . . . .
mimma šum-šu meš-ri- . . mâti . . . -šu
DINGIR - BIL - GI ZAGIN - NA . . . . GE
^{ilu} „ *el - lu nu - u - [ri] . . . . . . nim*
URUDU - GAR - LIG - GA ŠE - IR . . . .
„ *- u* . . . .
. . . SUR U ZI - G[A] . . . .
. . . *ma - na - ḫa - ti - šu na - piš - tu* . . . .
. . . . ME LA KIN GUD MA . . . . . .
. . . . . *ri ṣi - riš ra - biš a - na ši* . . .
. . . . *ti in - ni - ip - pu - uš*
[DINGIR-NUZKU] LUḪ-MAḪ NUN-GAL DINGIR-EN-KI-GE
[^{ilu}*Nuzku*] *sukkallu ṣi-ru ša ru-bi-e rabe(e)* ^{ilu}*E-a*
. . . . [AZAG] GA EŠ-MAḪ IM-ME-IN-GAB-GAB
. . . . . . *el - li bîti ṣi - ri u - ṣa - in - šu*

(PLATE V.)

. . . . . DINGIR - RI - E - NE - GE GIN - MA
. . . . *- a - ti šîr ilâni*^{pl} *u - ša - lik - šu*
. . . . MA DINGIR - EN - KI - GA - GE
. . . . *- e - ti ša* ^{ilu}*E - a*
[DINGIR-SILIG-MULU (?)]-ŠAR NAM-ŠUB BA-AN-SUM
[^{ilu}*Marduk* (?)] - *šip - tum id - di*
[NAM - ŠUB] ZU - AB - A U - ME - NI - SUM
[*ši - pat*] *ap - si - i i - di - ma*
[NAM - ŠUB] NUN - KI - GA U - ME - NI - SUM
[*ši - pat*] ^{alu}*Eridi i - di - ma*
[URUDU - GAR - LIG] - GA UR - SAG AN - NA - GE
[ZA - PA - RAM - ME] - NE - A - NI UTUG UR - UR - RI
[„ *-u ḳar-ra-du* ^{ilu}] *A-nim ša ina ri-gim me-lam-me-šu*

Whatever its name, the limbs . . . .

The Fire-god undefiled [whose] light (?) . . .

A meteorite [whose] flash (?) . . . . .

. . . his resting-place life . . . .

. . . in power and might for . . .

. . . . hath been made.

[Nuzku], supreme minister of the great prince Ea,

With pure . . . hath filled the lofty house,

(Plate V.)

Hath brought . . . the flesh of gods . . .

. . . . of Ea,

[Marduk (?)] hath performed the incantation;

Perform [the Incantation] of the Deep, and

Perform [the Incantation] of Eridu and

Take the potent meteorite of Heaven

[utukki] i - ar - ra - ru

. . . . GIDIM AB - SI - IL - LA

. . . . *[še] - e - du ud - da - pa - ru*

[Hiatus.]

RA . . . .

. . . .

LA - RA . . . .

pu - uš - ḳu . . . .

DINGIR-SILIG-MULU-ŠAR [IGI : GAR-GA-E : GIN-NA DU-MU]

SAḪ - TUR - RA . . . .

„ *- a* . . . .

SAG - MULU - TUR - RA - GE . . . .

ḳaḳ - ḳad mar - ṣi . . . .

LIKIR - BI : *lib - ba - šu u - su - uḫ* . . . . . .

MULU - TUR - RA SAG ŠA - GA - NA . . . . . .

ša mar - ṣi ina ri - [eš lib - bi - šu] . . . . .

MUD - BI DA GIŠ - NAD - DA - NA - GE . . . . .

da - mi - šu i - da - at ir - ši . . . .

SAḪ - TUR - RA ID - RIG - NE - NE [U] - ME - NI - RI - RI

„ *- a a - na meš - ri - ti - šu pur - ri - is - ma*

MUḪ MULU-TUR-RA-GE [:] *el mar-ṣi mu-uṣ-ṣi-ma*

Col. III.

MULU-GIŠGAL-LU-BI A-GUB-BA ZU-AB AZAG-GA

U - ME - NI - EL - LA[1] U - ME - NI - LAḪ - LAḪ - GA[1]

amelu šu - a - tu[2] *ina* „ *- e el - li ša ap - si - i*

ul - lil - šu ub - bi - ib - šu - ma

GAR - NA GIBILLA U - ME - NI - E

„ „ *- a šu - bi - ' - šu - ma*

At whose awful roar the spirits quake
. . . . . . a Demon hath removed

[Hiatus.]

. . . .
Misery . . . .
Marduk [hath seen; "What I"; "Go, my son (Marduk)"]
"[Take] a sucking-pig [and] . . . .
"[At] the head of the sick man [put it (?) and]
"Take out its heart and
"Above the heart of the sick man [put it],
"[Sprinkle] its blood on the sides of the bed [and]
"Divide the pig over his limbs and
"Spread it on the sick man; then

COL. III.

"Cleanse thou that man with pure water from the Deep
"And wash him clean and
"Bring near him a censer (and) a torch

---

[1] S. 217 omits.

[2] S. 217 and 79–7–8, 295, *tum* for *tu-um*.

(PLATE VI.)

GAR-NE GAR[1]-ḪAR-RA *VII*-A-DU-*II*-A-AN KA AŠ-A-AN U-ME-NI-PA-PA
a-kal tu-um[2]*-ri si-bit a-di ši-na*
bâb ka-me-e[3] *i-ta-as-suk-ma*
SAḪ-TUR-RA KI-BI-IN-GAR-RA-BI-KU U-ME-NI-SUM
„ *-a a-na pu-ḫi-šu i-din-ma*
UZU UZU-BI-KU MUD MUD-BI-KU U-ME-NI-SUM
ŠU-ḪA-BA-AB-TI[4]-GA
še[5]*-ra kima*[6] *se*[5]*-ri-šu da-me*[7] *kima*[6] *da-me-šu i-din-ma lil-ḳu-u*
LIKIR SAG ŠA-GA-NA-GE U-ME-NI-GAR
ŠA-GA-GIM U-ME-NI-SUM ŠU-ḪA-BA-AB-TI[4]-GA
lib-ba ša ina riš lib-bi-šu taš-ku-na
ki-ma lib-bi[8]*-šu i-din-ma lil-ḳu-u*
. . . . ḪUL GAL-LA RA-AḪ . .
. . . . SAR . .
. . . . *-nu*
. . . . *-su*

[1] 5,217 and 79–7–8, 295 omit.
[2] S. 217 and 79–7–8, 295, *tum* for *tu-um*.
[3] S. 217, *mi-i* for *me-e*.
[4] S. 217, *te*.
[5] S. 217, *ši*.
[6] S. 217, *ki-ma*.
[7] S. 217, *ma*.
[8] S. 217 omits.

[a] *Akal tumri.* Jensen suggests the meaning "Salz" for *tumri* as a synonym of *ṭâbtu* and *idranu* (*Mythen und Epen*, p. 447). However, a wider comparison of the texts in which it occurs will probably suggest a different meaning:

tarami-mu[am] re'u tabula, ša kainamma tumri išpukakki: "Thou didst love the shepherd Tabula (?), who perpetually heaped up *tumri* for thee." (Gilgamish, Tablet VI, 58–59.)

. . . . *imma nigittu ibteli išatu*, ... *imtaḳḳutu itur ana tumri*:

(PLATE VI.)

" Twice seven loaves cooked in the ashes [a] against
the shut door place and
" Give the pig in his stead and
" Let the flesh be as his flesh,
" And the blood as his blood,
" And let him hold it ;
" Let the heart be as his heart
" (Which thou hast placed upon his heart)
" And let him hold it ;
. . . .
. . . .

"The light [died away?], the fire went out, the . . . . [which] had fallen turned to *tumri*." (Gilgamish, S. 1,040, ll. 19–20; Jensen, *Mythen*, p. 164.)

ina napḫar matati-ki išatu iddi-ma kima tumri išpuk: "On all thy lands he hath cast fire and like *tumri* hath heaped up." (*W.A.I.*, iv, 19, No. 3, 40.)

širu ša ina penti bašlu akal tumri ul ikkal: "Flesh which hath been cooked on the coals, bread of *tumri* shall he not eat." (*W.A.I.*, iv, 32, ii, 15)

kaman tumri (Craig, *Religious Texts*, 15, 20, K. 2,001): "a cake of *tumri*."

Akal tumri sibit adi šina bab kamê itassuk-ma: "Twice seven loaves of *tumri* place against the closed door." (This passage.)

A vocabulary gives a group *tu-um-*[*ru*], *ki-nu-nu* ("oven"), and *ḳu-tu-ru* (connected with *ḳutru*, "smoke"), (K. 13,690). From these it seems fairly clear that *tumru* means "ashes," the "bread of ashes" being the ordinary flat cake such as is cooked in the ashes by the Arabs of the present day.

. . . KI - BI - IN - [GAR - RA - BI - KU] . . . . .
. . . *lu - u pu - [u - ḫi - šu]* . . . .
[SAḪ - TUR] - RA GAR - SAG - IL - LA - BI . . . .
[„] - *u lu - u di - na - [ni - šu]* . . . . . .
UTUG-ḪUL A-LA-ḪUL BAR-KU HE-IM-TA-[GUB]
UTUG- * ŠIG-GA ALAD- * ŠIG-GA ḪE-EN-DA-LAḪ-LAḪ-[GI-EŠ]

INIM - INIM - MA SAḪ - TUR - RA . . . .

EN[1] AZAG-GIG-GA SU MULU KA-MU-UN-GAL-[LA]
a-šak-ku mar-ṣu ina zu-mur ameli it-tab-ši
MULU-GIŠGAL-LU PAP-ḪAL-LA TU-GIM BA-AN-DUL
amelu mut-tal-li-ka[2] *ki-ma ṣu-ba-ti ik-ta-tam*
ŠU - BI GIR - BI NU - MU - UN - ŠI - IN - GA - GA
ḳa - as[3] *- su u še - ip - šu i - na - aš - ši*
ID - ŠU - GIR - BI [MU - UN - ŠI - IN] - GE - GE
meš - ri - ti - šu u - ta - ra
NUN - GAL DINGIR - EN - KI - GE EN - ZU . . . .
ru - bu - u ra - bu - u ilu *E - a bêl šip - ti*
DINGIR - EN - KI - E - NE - KU . . . .
ša [ ] ilu „
* BIR SAG GAB - RI - [BI - KU BA - AN - SUM]
u-ri-[ṣa ina riši-šu] ana mi-ḫir-ti-šu it-ta-din
NUN - ME - E GU - NA[M - M]I - IN - DE
ana ab - kal - li is - si - ma
* BIR GAR-SAG-IL-LA NAM-MULU-GIŠGAL-LU-GE
(15). *u - ri - ṣu „ - u ša a - me - lu - ti*

[That the] . . . may be in his stead . . .

25. [That the] pig may be a substitute for him . . .

May the evil Spirit, the evil Demon stand aside!

May a kindly Spirit, a kindly Genius be present!

Prayer of the Sucking-Pig.

Incantation :—

30. An evil Fever rests upon the body of the man,

It hath covered the wanderer as with a garment,

It holdeth his hands and feet,

35. It racketh his limbs.

The great Prince Ea, lord of magic,

40. Of Ea (?) . . . .

(11). Laid a kid at his head in front of him

Unto the Chieftain he spake (saying):

(15). "The kid is the substitute for mankind.

---

[1] The restorations are from Tablet "Z," *Cun. Texts*, part xvii, pl. xxxvii.

[2] K. 2,375, *ku*.

[3] K. 2,375, *ḳat*, K. 4,996, *ḳa* for *ḳa-as*.

*BIR ZI - A - NI - KU BA - AN - SUM
u - ri - ṣa ana na - piš - ti - šu it - ta - din
SAG *BIR SAG - MULU - KU BA - AN - SUM
ḳaḳ-ḳad u-ri-ṣi ana ḳaḳ-ḳad ameli it-ta-din
GU *BIR GU - MULU - KU BA - AN - SUM
ki-šad u-ri-ṣi ana ki-šad ameli it-ta-din
GABA *BIR GABA - MULU - KU BA - AN - SUM
ir - ti u - ri - ṣi ana ir - ti ameli it - ta - din
. . . . [MULU - KU] BA - AN - SUM
. . . . . . [*ana* . . . . *ameli*] *it - ta - din*
[TU-KA-GA I DINGIR-EN-KI-GA-GE: *ina* „]-*e a-mat* ilu *E-a*
[TU-TU ZU-AB NUN-KI-GA NAM]-MU-UN-DA-AN-BUR-RA
[*ši - pat ap - si - i* alu *Eridi a - a ip*] - *pa - ši - ir*

[Hiatus.]

COL. IV (PLATE VII).

UTUG - ḪUL - IK MULU - RA . . . .
u-tuk-ku lim-nu ša ameli . . . .
A-LA-ḪUL-IK NIM-GIR-GIM MU-UN-[GIR-GIR-RI]
a-lu-u lim-nu ša ki-ma bir-ḳi it-ta-nab-[*riḳ*]
GIDIM-ḪUL-IK MULU-RA ŠU . . . .
e - kim - mu lim - nu ša ameli im - [*ḫaṣ* ?]
MULLA ḪUL-IK MULU-RA MU (?) . . . . . .
gal-lu-u lim-nu ša ameli im-tu . . . . . .
E - NE - NE - NE MULU - KIN - GA - A . . . . . .
šu - nu mâr šip - ri lim - nu - [*ti šu - nu*]
DINGIR-EN-LIL-LA NU-*ŠUG-GA NAM-BI-KU-NE . . .
ilu „ *la še-ma-a a-na šim-*[*ti-šu*] . . . . .
IGI - BI - KU UR - NU - TUK SU . . . .
ana pa-ni-šu-nu la a-da-ru ina [*zumri* (?)] . . .

"The kid for his life he giveth,
"The head of the kid for the head of the man he giveth,
"The neck of the kid for the neck of the man he giveth,
"The breast of the kid for the breast of the man he giveth,
"The . . . [of the kid for the . . . of the man] he giveth,[a]
"By the magic of the Word of Ea
"[Let the Incantation of the Deep of Eridu never] be unloosed!"

[Hiatus.]

COL. IV (PLATE VII).

The evil Spirit which [hath seized upon] the man,
The evil Demon which flasheth like lightning,
The evil Ghost which hath smitten the man,
The evil Devil which . . . the man.
Fell harbingers are they!
Bel, [who destroyeth?] the senseless with his decree,
Feareth them not . . . . . .

---

[a] It is uncertain how many more of the lines ending "he giveth" were originally in the text.

EŠ - E - KUR - TA E - A - NE - NE - GE . . . .
iš-tu bît Ekurri ina a-ṣi-šu-nu . . . .
ḪU (?) - ṢAB (?) - ZI - GA - GIM . . . .
ki - ma ti - bu - tu e - ri - bi . . . .
GAR - ḪUL - ĬK - E MULU - RA BA . . . .
mimma lim-nu [ana ameli] . . . .
a - šak - ku e - . . . .
MULU - GIŠGAL - LU - BI . . . .
a - me - lu šu - [a - tu] . . . .
. . . .

[Col. V entirely lost.]

Col. VI.

. . . .
. . . . DIR DIR . . . .
. . . . GUB-BA-GIM AN . . . .
. . . . UD-DA KUD-DA-GIM . . . . . .

INIM - INIM - MA GAR - KIL . . . . . .

EN U - GAL DINGIR EDIN - NA . . . .
ID - BI - E - NE . . . .
MULU (?) EN-NUN-E-NE IN . . . .
KA - BI - E - NE IK - KID . . . .
KA - ŠA - AN DA - ŠA - A . . . .
. . . NAM NU - KID - KID . . . .

When they issued forth from the Underworld . .
Like a swarm of locusts . . . . . .
All evil against man . . . .
Fever . . . .
That man . . . .
. . . .

[Col. V entirely lost.]

COL. VII (PLATE VIII).

. . . .

. . . . NE SUM (?) . . . .

. . . . MU - UN - T[AK]

. . . . MU - UN - TAK

. . . . EL - LA MU - UN - TAK

. . . . DINGIR - RA - NA

. . . . TAK

ŠU - NA . . . .

MU - UN - EL - LA . . . .

EME - ḪUL - IK BAR - [KU ḪE - IM - TA - GUB]

INIM - INIM - MA A - SIG - GA (?) . . .

EN - UTUG - ḪUL EDIN - NA - ZU - KU

u - tuk - ku lim - nu

a - na ṣi - ri - ka

A - LA - ḪUL EDIN - NA - ZU - KU

a - lu - u lim - nu

a - na ṣi - ri - ka

GIDIM - ḪUL EDIN - NA - ZU - KU

e - kim - mu lim - nu

a - na ṣi - ri - ka

MULLA - ḪUL EDIN - NA - ZU - KU

gal - lu - u lim - nu a - na ṣi - ri - [*ka*]

. . . .

[Eleven lines of colophon remain in Col. VIII.]

COL. VII (PLATE VIII).

12. Incantation :—

O evil Spirit! To thy desert!

15. O evil Demon! To thy desert!

20. O evil Ghost! To thy desert!

O evil Devil! To thy desert!

[Remainder lost.]

The Eleventh Tablet.

(Plate IX.)

EN AZAG MULU-RA SAG-BI MU-UN-NA-[TE]
a-šak-ku a-na ameli a-na ḳaḳ-ḳa-di-šu it-te-ḫi
NAM-TAR MULU-RA ZI-BI MU-UN-NA-TE
nam-ta-ru a-na[1] *ameli a-na na-piš-ti-šu it-te-ḫi*
UTUG-ḪUL GU-BI MU-UN-NA-TE
u-tuk-ku lim-nu a-na[1] *ki-[ša-di]-šu it-te-ḫi*
A-LA-ḪUL GABA-BI [MU]-UN-NA-TE
a-lu-u lim-nu a-na[1] *ir-ti-šu it-te-ḫi*
GIDIM-ḪUL IB-BI MU-UN-NA-TE
e-kim-mu lim-nu a-na ḳab-li-šu it-te-ḫi
MULLA-ḪUL ŠU-BI MU-UN-NA-TE
gal-lu-u lim-nu a-na ḳa-ti-šu it-te-ḫi
DINGIR-ḪUL GIR-BI MU-UN-NA-TE
ilu lim-nu a-na še-pi-šu it-te-ḫi
VII-BI-E-NE UR-BI-A BA-AN-DIB-BI-EŠ
si-bit-ti-šu-nu ištениš(niš) iṣ-ṣab-tu-uš
BAR-BI-TA[2] BIL-BIL-LA-GIM BA-AB . . . UŠ
zu-mur-šu kima i-ša-ti ḫum-mu-du uš-tam (?) . . . *-u*
GAR-ŠA-A GAR-ḪUL-GIM-MA BA- . . . . . . -UŠ
ki-ma e-piš limuttim(tim) . . . . . . *-šu*
TU-GIM BA-AN-DUL . . . . BARA
DINGIR-SILIG-MULU-ŠAR IGI-IM-MA-AN-[SUM: GAR-GA-E: GIN-NA D]U-MU
*BIR-GIG-IB GABA-BI . . . . E
u-ri-ṣa ṣal-ma ša ḳab-la [na-as]-ḫu

The Eleventh Tablet.

(Plate IX.)

Incantation :—

Fever unto the man, against his head, hath drawn nigh,
Disease unto the man, against his life, hath drawn nigh,
An evil Spirit against his neck hath drawn nigh,
An evil Demon against his breast hath drawn nigh,
An evil Ghost against his belly hath drawn nigh,
An evil Devil against his hand hath drawn nigh,
An evil God against his foot hath drawn nigh,
These seven together have seized upon him,
His body like a consuming fire they devour (?),
As one that worketh evil they have . . . him,
As with a garment they envelop him . . .
Marduk hath seen him : (etc.),
" What I " : (etc.),
" Go, my son,
" [Take] a dark-coloured kid whose stomach [hath been taken away],

---

1 K. 9,406, *ana* for *a-na*.

2 K. 5,210 omits.

LU ID - DAR - A GIR - BI . . . . E
im - mir at - ri - e . . . . - ḫa
SU U - ME - NI . . . . [U - ME] - NI - E
maš - ka ta - . . . . [tu] - šaḫ - ḫaṭ
ŠU GIR *SIG - ALAM . . . [U] - ME - NI - GAR - GAR
. . . . *ta - ša - kan*
MULU - TUR - [RA][1] . . . . . [U] - ME - NI - GUB
. . . . U - ME - NI - E
. . . . *-a zi - mi - šu tu - ḫal - lap*
. . . . U - ME - NI - E
. . . . *da mi ta šu ma*
. . . . . NA RIG-LI RIG-ZUN U-ME-NI-BIL-BIL
šu-ru-up-ma
. . . . SI - IM - E - NE

(PLATE X.)

. . . . *šu - ṣi - in - šu - ma*
. . . . BA - AB - SIR - RI
. . . . *i - na - as - sa - ḫu*
. . . . ḪA - BA - RA - GUB - BA
[UTUG-ḪUL A-LA-ḪUL BAR-KU ḪE]-IM-TA-GUB
[UTUG-*ŠIG-GA ALAD-*ŠIG-GA ḪE-EN]-LAḪ-LAḪ-GI-EŠ

. . . . A - GE

[EN AZ]AG MULU - RA IMI - GIM BA - AN - RI
[a-šak]-ku a-na ameli ki-ma ša-a-ri i-zik-ma
[MULU - BI] . . NE - IN - RA SA - TI - BI BA - AN - TU
[amelu šu (?)]-a-tum im-ḫa-aṣ-ma ba-ma-as-su im-ši-id
[IGI - BI] BA - AN - GAZ SA - GU - BI BA - AN - RA - AḪ
[pa (?)] - ni - šu im - ḫaṣ - ma la - ba - an - šu i - ti - iḳ

25. " A fat[a] lamb whosė leg [hath been taken away]
" [Thou shalt flay off] the skin, thou shalt tear away the . . . .
30. " Hand and foot (?) an image . . . thou shalt set
" The sick man . . . . thou shalt place
" . . . . thou shalt cover his face
35. " . . . .
" burn . . . . . . cypress and herbs (?)

(Plate X.)

" . . . . fill it
40. " [That the great gods] may remove [the evil ?],
" [That the evil Spirit] may stand aside,
" [May the evil Spirit, the evil Demon] stand aside,
" [May a kindly Spirit, a kindly Genius] be present."

[Prayer . . . .]

---

45. [Incantation :—]
Fever hath blown upon the man as the wind-blast,
It hath smitten this man, and humbled his pride,
50. It hath smitten his . . . and hath brought him low,

---

[1] K. 5,210 translates [*a-me*]-*lu* . . . .

[a] *Atru* usually means "abundant."

[ ] GIM SA-BI BA-AN-SUR-SUR
[*kima pa*]-*ti-in-ni bu-a-ni-šu u-te-en-niš*
[KA-BI] ṢI-KU BA-AN-TU A MUḪ-BI NU-UN-DUG
[*pi*(?)]-*i-šu a-na mar-ti it-tur mu-u eli-šu ul ṭa-a-bu*
. . . [ID-ŠU]-GIR-BI NU-UN-DA-GI
. . . . [*meš-ri-ti-šu*] *ul u-tar*
. . . . -UN-DA-ŠA-A
. . . . *ili-šu*
. . . . *i-li-'*
. . . . -*ḫi-ip*
. . . . -GUB-BU
. . . . -*za-az*

[Hiatus.]

. . . .
. . . . -*raš-šu*
. . . . -TAR-RI
. . . . -*ri-šu*
MULU-GIŠGAL-LU U [NU-UN-DA-AB-KU-E A NU-UN]-DA-AB-NAK-E
U-NU-MU̧-UN-KU-KU [ ]-ZI-ZI
ul i-ṣal-lal u[*l*] *u-šap-šiḫ*
DINGIR-RA-A-NI ZI-MU-UN-ŠI-[IN]-IR-IR-RI
ili-šu u-ta-aš-ši-iš
DINGIR-SILIG-MULU-ŠAR IGI : GAR-GA-E : GIN-NA DU-MU
* BIR BABBAR DINGIR-EN-MIR-SI-GE ŠU-U-ME-TI
„ *piṣu*(*u*) *ša* ^{ilu}*Dumu-zi* ˙ *li-ḳi-ma*
(Plate XI.)
TE MULU-TUR-RA-GE U-ME-NI-[NA]
ina ṭi-iḫ mar-ṣi šu-ni-il-ma

It hath rotted his thews like a girdle,[a]
His mouth it hath turned to gall
So that the moisture therein hath no sweetness,
55. . . . . . . so that he cannot move his limbs,
. . . . his god (?)
. . . . he hath [no] power,
60. . . . . destroying (?)
. . . . standeth
. . . .

[Hiatus.]

67. The man [can eat no] food, [no water can he] drink,
He cannot sleep, he hath no rest,
70. His god hath let him be brought low.
Marduk hath seen him : (etc.),
"What I" : (etc.),
"Go, my son (Marduk),
"Take a white kid of Tammuz,

(PLATE XI.)

75. "Lay it down facing the sick man and

---

[a] Cf. Jer., xiii, 1 ff.

LIKIR - A - NI U - ME - NI - [SIR]

lib - ba - šu u - suḫ - ma

ŠU MULU - BÁ - GE U - ME - NI - GAR

ana ḳa - ti ameli šu - a - ti šu - kun - ma

NAM - ŠUB NUN - KI - GA U - ME - NI - SUM

*BIR ṆI ŠA-BI U-MUS-TA-E-ZI GAR-GAR-LAG-GA

MULU - BA - GE U - MU - UN - TE - GUR - GUR

u - ri - ṣa ša libbi - šu ta - as - su - ḫu

a-ka-la li-i ša amelu šu-a-tu kup-pir-ma

GAR - NA GIBILLA U - ME - NI - E

SILA - KU U - ME - NI - DUB - DUB - BU

MULU - GIŠGAL - LU - BI KU - SUR - RA U - ME - ḪAR

amelu šu - a - ti ku - sur - ra - a e - ṣir - ma

NAM-ŠUB NUN-KI-GA U-ME-NI-SUM : ZI DINGIR-
GAL-GAL-E-NE-GE U-ME-NI-PA

UTUG - ḪUL A - LA - ḪUL GIDIM - ḪUL

DINGIR - RAB - KAN - ME DINGIR - RAB - KAN - ME - A

AZAG NAM-TAR DUGUD SU MULU-GIŠGAL NI-GAL-LI

ḪU - MU - RA - AB - ZI - ZI E - TA ḪA - BA - RA - E

li - in - na - si - iḫ iš - tu bîti lit - ta - ṣi

UTUG - * ŠIG - GA ALAD - * ŠIG - GA ḪE - EN - DA - LAḪ-
LAḪ-GI-EŠ

UTUG - ḪUL A - LA - ḪUL GIDIM - ḪUL

"Take out its heart and
"Place it in the hand of that man;
"Perform the Incantation of Eridu,
"The kid whose heart thou hast taken out
"Is *li'i*[a]-food with which thou shalt make an 'atonement' for the man,
"Bring forth a censer (and) a torch,
"Scatter it in the street,
"Bind a bandage on that man,
"Perform the Incantation of Eridu,
"Invoke the great gods
"That the evil Spirit, the evil Demon, evil Ghost,
"Hag-demon, Ghoul,
"Fever, or heavy Sickness
"Which is in the body of the man,
"May be removed and go forth from the house!
"May a kindly Spirit, a kindly Genius be present!"
O evil Spirit! O evil Demon! O evil Ghost!

---

[a] *Li'i*, at present quite unknown. It occurs elsewhere in the line GAR-GAR-LIG-GA SAG-GA-NA U-ME-NI-GAR (i.e. *akala lî ina ḳaḳḳadi-šu šukun-ma*), Tablet "T," l. 38, and *lî ša ina zumri kuppuru*, *W.A.I.*, ii, 17, 65.

DINGIR - RAB - KAN - ME DINGIR - RAB - KAN - ME - A

ŠA - GIG LIKIR - GIG SAG - GIG KA - GIG

mu-ru-uṣ lib-bi ki-iṣ lib-bi mu-ru-uṣ ḳaḳ-ḳa-di „ *šin-ni*

AZAG NAM - TAR DUGUD

nam - ta - ru a - šak - ku kab - tum

ZI AN - NA - KI - BI - RA - GE U - UN - NE - PA

INIM - INIM - MA * BIR - ḪUL - DUB - BA - GE

EN AZAG EN-TE-NA-GIM KALAM-MA MU-UN-ZI

Duppu XI^{KAM} EN AZAG - GIG - GA - MEŠ

[Colophon.]

O Hag-demon! O Ghoul!
O Sickness of the heart! O Heartache!
O Headache! O Toothache!
O Pestilence! O grievous Fever!
By Heaven and Earth may ye be exorcised!

PRAYER OF THE KID AS SUBSTITUTE (?).

Incantation:—"Fever like frost hath come upon the land."

ELEVENTH TABLET OF THE SERIES "SICK FEVER."

The Twelfth Tablet.

OBVERSE.

(PLATE XXVII.)

[EN AZAG EN-TE-NA]-GIM KALAM-MA MU-UN-ZI
[a-šak-ku kima ku]-uṣ-ṣi a-na ma-a-ti it-te-ba-a
. . . . . . [GIM] KI-A IM-MI-IN-A-AN
. . . . . *[kima na]-al-ši ina irṣitim(tim) ina-al-lu-uš*
. . . . NE-IN-DUL
. . . . *kima za-ma-nu i-kat-tam*
. . . . NE-IN-UL
. . . . *kima al-pi i-na-kap*
. . . . IN-GUL-LA
. . . . *ri i-ab-bat*
. . . . GIR-GIR-RI
. . . . *bir-ḳi it-ta-nab-ri-ḳu*
. . . . GAR NU-TUK-A
. . . . *-ma-ra ul i-ši*
. . . . GIN-GIN-A-NI-TA
. . . . *ina a-la-ki-šu-nu*
. . . . KI-A IN-TUDKI-E-NE
. . . . *-gi-me irṣitim(tim) u-na-aš-šu*
. . . . GAN-KU AB-ŠA-ŠA-E
. . . . *i-ḫab-bi-lu*
. . . . * SIG-GA BA-AN-GAR-RI-EŠ
. . . . *ša-ḳu-um-ma-tu iš-ku-nu*
. . . . GIM MU-UN-DIB-DIB-BI-EŠ
. . . . *ki-ma mê*^{pl} *miṭ-ri u-ṣab-bi-tum*

The Twelfth Tablet.

OBVERSE.

(PLATE XXVII.)

[Incantation]:—

[Fever] like frost hath come upon the land,
.. . . like a rainstorm hath rained upon the earth,
. . . . like an enemy (?) covereth,
. . . . . like a bull rusheth loose,
. . . . destroyeth
. . . . . . [like] lightning flasheth
. . . . hath no . . .
. . . . in their path,
. . . . . . they make the earth to quake,
. . . . . . they bring to destruction,
. . . . they cause woe,
. . . . . like rain (?)-waters they have seized

. . . . RA-GIM MU-UN-DIB-DIB-BI-EŠ
. . . . [*ki-ma*] *nu-un ap-si-i i-bar-ru*
. . . . MU-UN-DIB-DIB-BI-EŠ
. . . . *-tak-ka-ni i-kam-mu-u*
. . . . MU - UN - DIB - DIB - BI - EŠ
[*id - lu ina* (?) *ma*] *- ḫa - zi i - kam - mu - u*
. . . . MU - UN - DIB - DIB - BI - EŠ
[*ar - da - tu ina* (?)] *maš - ta - ki - ša i - kam - mu - u*
. . . . DI DINGIR-NINNI(NI)-TA MU-UN-DIB-DIB-BI-EŠ
. . . . *a - šar me - lul - ti i - kam - mu - u*
. . . . RA GAB - IM - MA - AN - RI - EŠ
. . . . *bel ilâni*^pl^ *im - taḫ - ru - ma*
. . . . [A - LA] - GIM IM - MI - IN - DUL
. . . . [*ki*] *- ma a - li - e ik - ta - tam - šu*

(Plate XXVIII.)

. . . . GIM IM - MI - IN - ŠU
. . . . *ri i - sa - ḫap - šu*
. . . . RA NE - IN - RA
. . . . *ti it - tar - šu*
. . . . NE - IN - DE
. . . . *e it - ta - ḳi*
. . . . GUB - BU - UŠ

[Hiatus.]

[*ina ua umešam*] *uš - ta - bar - ri*
[DINGIR - SILIG - MULU - ŠAR : GAR - GA - E :] GIN - NA
. . . . U - ME - NI - SIR
. . . . *u - suḫ - ma*
. . . . TA U - ME - NI - GAR
. . . . *šu šu - kun - ma*

. . . . . like a fish of the Ocean they chase,
. . . . they seize upon,
[The hero in ?] the fortress they seize upon,
[The maid in ?] her chamber they seize upon,
. . . . . . a place of delight they seize upon.
They come before . . . the lord of the gods and
. . . covereth him like a demon

(PLATE XXVIII.)

. . . . . like . . . it overwhelmeth him
. . . . it turneth him
. . . . it slayeth him

[Hiatus.]

[With cries of woe daily] is he sated.
[Marduk hath seen, etc. ;]
[" What I," etc. ;]
" Go, my son (Marduk),
" Take out the . . . . . . and
" Lay it on his . . . . and

. . . . . DUB-BA KI-NA-A-NI-TA U-ME-NI-DUL
. . . *a ina ma-a-a-li-šu kut-tim-šu-ma*
. . . . GAR-NA EL-LA GAR-NA RI-GA
. . . ṢIR KISAL-ERIN-NA LAL NI-NUN-NA MUḪ-BI U-ME-NI-DE
. . . . *ša-man ru-uš-ti ša-man* ^*iṣu*^ *e-ri-ni*
[*diš-pu*] *ḫi-me-tu eli-šu šu-ru-up-ma*
[NAM-ŠUB NUN-KI-G]A U-ME-NI-SUM
[*ši-pat* ^*alu*^]*Eridi i-di-ma*
. . . BA SU MULU-GIŠGAL-LU PAP-ḪAL-LA-TA TUM-A
. . . . [*ina zumur*] *ameli mut-tal-li-ki ta-bal-ma*
. . . . [*ultu* (?)] *bîti* (?) *šu-ṣi-ma* : E-DA-A-NI-TA
[UTUG-ḪUL ALAD]-ḪUL BAR-KU ḪE-IM-TA-GUB
[UTUG-*ŠIG-GA ALAD]-*ŠIG-GA ḪE-EN-DA-LAḪ-LAḪ-GI-EŠ

[INIM-INIM-MA] . . . SU BIR-ḪUL-DUB-BA MULU-TUR-RA DUL-LA

. . . . A KIN-GA-A AŠ-GE-GE

[*Duppi XII*^KAM-MA^ EN AZAG]-GIG-GA-MEŠ

[Colophon.]

" With . . . on his bed cover him and
" . . . . with a censer cleanse, with a censer purify.
" And burn thereon oil of balsam (?),[a] oil of cedar,
" Honey and butter, and
" Perform [the Incantation] of Eridu,
" Remove the . . . from the body of the wanderer and
" Put it outside the house
" [May the evil Spirit, the evil Genius] stand aside,
" [May a kindly Spirit], a kindly [Guardian] be present!"

[PRAYER OF] COVERING THE SICK MAN WITH THE BODY (?) OF THE KID AS SUBSTITUTE (?).

. . . . messenger . . . (?)

[TWELFTH TABLET] OF THE SERIES "[FEVER] SICKNESS."

[Colophon.]

[a] *Rušṭu* (also in l. 42 of Tablet VIII of the series *Luḫ-ka*) possibly to be connected with the Chaldee *riḫuš* (Levy, *Chald. Wörterb.*, p. 420, *a*).

Series "Ṭi'i."

The Third Tablet.

OBVERSE.

(PLATE XII.)

EN SAG-GIG GU-SA-A-AN [: *ṭi-ḫi*]-*i mu-tum a-ḫi da-da-nu* : GU-SA . . .

SAG-GIG IGI-BI-TA : *ṭi-ḫi-i*[1] *ina pa-ni-šu im-tu i-sa-ri* : UḪ (?) IM-TA . . .

SAG-GIG E-KUR-TA : *ṭi-ḫi-i*[1] *iš-tu ekurri it-ta-ṣa-a* : NAM-[TA-E]

E DINGIR-EN-LIL-LA-TA : *iš-tu bît* ^{ilu}*Bêl it-ta-ṣa-a* : NAM-[TA-E]

KUR-RA KUR-ŠA-TA : *iš-tu ki-rib ša-di-i*[2] *ana ma-a-tum*[3] *ur-du*[4] : NAM-TA-[GIBIŠ-NE]

GIL-ḪAR-SAG-GA-TA : *iš-tu kip-pat ša-di-i*[2] *ana ma-a-tum*[3] *ur-du*[4] : KUR-RA NAM-TA-GIBIŠ-[NE]

AGAR NU-GA-GA-A-TA : *iš-tu u-ga-ri ana la*[5]-*ta-a*[6]-*ri ur-du*[4] : NAM-TA-GIBIŠ-NE

SIḲḲA[7]-KI TUR-TA : *it-ti*[8] *šap-pa-ri ana tar-ba-ṣu ur-du*[4] : NAM-TA-GIBIŠ-NE

DARA SI-ḪAL-ḪAL-LA-TA : *it-ti*[8] *tu-ra-ḫu*[9] *ana ḳar-nu*[10] *pi-ta-a-tu*[11] *ur-du*[4] : NAM-TA-GIBIŠ-NE

Series "Headache."

The Third Tablet.

OBVERSE.

(PLATE XII.)

Incantation :—

Headache [a]

Headache—in its face venom putrefieth.[b]

Headache hath come forth from the Underworld,

It hath come forth from the Dwelling of Bel,

From amid the mountains it hath descended upon the land,

From the ends of the mountains it hath descended upon the land,

From the fields not to return it hath descended ;

With the mountain-goat unto the fold it hath descended,

With the ibex unto the Open-horned (flocks) it hath descended,

---

[1] 91,011, *ḫu* for *ḫi-i*.
[2] 91,011, *šadi*.
[3] 91,011, *mâti* for *ma-a-tum*.
[4] 91,011, *da*.
[5] 91,011 adds *a*.
[6] 91,011 omits.
[7] 91,011 inserts BAR.
[8] 91,011, *iš-tu*.
[9] 91,011, *ḫi*.
[10] 91,011, *ni*.
[11] 91,011, *ta*.

[a] The sense of this line is not clear, and the word *dadanu* is of unknown meaning. It may, however, be referred to the root *dâdu*, Syraic *dawwed*, "to disturb" (Payne Smith, 823).

[b] *isari*, Syriac *s'ri*, Brockelmann, *Lexicon*, p. 239*a*.

SI-BAR-RA SI-GUL-GUL-LA-TA NAM-TA-GIBIŠ-NE
iš-tu ḳar-nu[1] *pi-ta-a-tu*[2] *ana ḳar-nu*[1]
rab-ba-a-[*tu*][2] *ur-*[*du*][3]

IGI-BI-TA GIN-GIN-NI : *ina ma-ḫar tal-*[*lak*]*-ti-šu*
ša-ḳu-u-ti : U-IL-LA

[GUD]-NA-A : *al-pi ša rab-ṣa al-pi u*[4]*-kas-si* :
GUD-E BA-LAL

. . . UD : *ku-um-mu u-ma-al-la*[5] : IM-* DIRIG-GA

. . . LA MU-UN-NA-AN-TE-EŠ U-GIM MU . . .

. . . . *iṭ-ḫi-e-ma ki-ma ûmi*(*mi*) . . . .

. . . . E . . A . . . .

. . . . GE-GE DINGIR-EN-KI . . . .

. . . *an-nu-u ṭe-e-*[*mu* ^{ilu}]*Ea* . . . . . .

. . . RA : *a-na a-bi-šu* . . . *a-mat šu-a-*[*tu*] . . .

. . . AB-GE-GE-E . . . .

. . . *šup-šu-ḫi-ka ia-a-tu* . . . .

[A-NA] IB-BA ŠA-A-I (?) : *mi-na-a i-*[*pa*]*-šu-u ia-a-tu* . . .

[DINGIR-EN]-KI DU-NI DINGIR-SILIG-MULU-ŠAR :
^{ilu}*Ea ma-ri-šu* ^{ilu}*Marduk ip-*[*pal*
MU-UN-NA-NI-IB-GE-GE]

[DU-MU A-N]A NU-NI-ZU : *ma-ri mi-na-a la ti-i-di*
mi-na-a [*lu-uṣ-ṣip-ka* : A-NA RA-AB-DAḪ-A]

[DINGIR-SILIG-MULU-ŠAR A-NA] NU-NI-ZU : ^{ilu}*Marduk*
mi-na-a la ti-i-di [*mi-na-a lu-rad-di-ka* : A-NA
RA-AB-DAḪ-A]

[GAR-GA-E-NI] ZU-A-MU : *ša a-na-ku i-du-u at-ta*
ti-i-di : [ZA-E IN-GA-E-ZU]

[GIN-NA] DU-MU : *a-lik ma-ri* ^{ilu}*Marduk* : DINGIR-
[SILIG-MULU-ŠAR]

With the Open-horned unto the Big-horned it hath descended.
Before its overbearing course
An ox seizeth upon its fellow which coucheth.[a]
It filleth the dwelling-place,
It hath drawn nigh . . . . and like a storm . . .
. . . .
[Marduk] this as a report [unto his father] Ea related,
Unto his father [he brought] this word :
" By thine assuaging . . . .
" What I am to do [I know not]."
Ea made answer unto his son Marduk :
" O my son, what dost thou not know ?
" What [more can I give thee] ?
" O Marduk, what dost thou not know ?
" [What can I add unto thy knowledge ?]
" What I know, thou knowest also.
" Go, my son Marduk,

[1] 91,011, *ni*.
[2] 91,011, *ta*.
[3] 91,011, *da*.
[4] 91,011, *i*.
[5] 91,011, *li*.

[a] Doubtful line: *ukassi* apparently has the sense of "catching," and is used of oxen elsewhere: cf. the Story of Etana (Zimmern, *Mythen und Epen*, 104, l. 17), *uktassika ri*[*ma mîtu*].

. . . . ZU : *mu-di-e al-ka-ka-a-te a-lik mu-di-e al-ka-ka-a-*[*te* : GIN-NA . . . . ZU]

[NI LID-AZAG-GA GA]-LID-TUR-MA : *šam-ni ar-ḫi el-li-ti ša ši-zib la-a-tu li-ḳi-e-*[*ma* : ŠU-U-ME-TI]

. . . NAM-ŠUB NUN-KI-GA NA-RI-GA U-ME-[NI-SUM]

. . . *-i ši-pat* ^{alu}*Eridi šip-tum ellitim*(*tim*) *i-di-šum-*[*ma*]

. . . ŠU]-*UR-RA-A-NI BAR-RA-A-NI ŠU-ŠED-DA . .

. . . . *-ti te-'-šu pu-uš-šu-uḫ-*[*ma*]

REVERSE.

(PLATE XIII.)

. . . . *iz-zu ša ilâni*^{pl} : ŠUR-RA DINGIR-RI-E-[NE]

. . . *ḫuš-gal-la ša* ^{ilu}*Bêl e-ṭi-ru* : IN-DA . . .

. . . *ša* ^{ilu}*Gu-la u* ^{ilu}*Nin-ni si*(?)*-in* . . .

. . . *iḳ-ḳu-lu ba-nu-u iš-tu mâti-šu ib-bab-la* : KUR . . .

. . . . RI-E ḪAR-TA BA . . . .

. . . . *sab*(?) *-ḫi*(?) *i* . . . .

. . . . *ar* . . *a u-kas-su* . . . .

. . . . *meš-ri-ti-šu ša-aš-ša-ṭu* . . . .

. . . . NA-GE IM-TE-NA . . . . . .

. . . . A-NI ḪE . . . .

. . . . *ba-'-* . . . .

. . . . *-a-tu* . . . *li* . . . .

[*VII*-NA-MEŠ *si-bit-t*]*i šu-nu si-bit-ti šu-nu VII*-NA-[MEŠ]

IDIM-ZU-AB-[TA *i*]*-na na-ḳab ap-si-i si-bit-ti šu-nu VII*-NA-[MEŠ]

" O thou cunning in device,
" Go, O thou cunning in device,
" Take the fat of an undefiled cow,
" And the milk of kine,
" Perform for him . . . . the Incantation of Eridu, the pure Incantation,
" Assuage his pain (?) and

REVERSE.

(PLATE XIII.)

" The angry . . . . of the gods,
" The . . . which Bel preserved
" . . . . of Gula and Ninni . . . .
" . . . a pure . . . hath been brought from his mountain,
" . . . .
" . . . his limbs . . . .
. . . .
. . . .

Seven are they, seven are they,
In the depth of Ocean seven are they,

NUN-KI-GA *VII*-NA-MEŠ ŠU-LAL DINGIR-EN-KI-GE *VII*-NA-MEŠ

ina [*alu*]*Eridi si-bit-ti šu-nu mu-kas-su-u ša* [*ilu*]*E-a si-bit-ti šu-nu*

E - NE - NE - NE ZU - AB - TA E - [A] - MEŠ

šu - nu iš - tu ap - si - i it - ta - ṣu - ni šu - nu

U - MU - UN - HUL[1] UB - TA . . . LAḪ - LAḪ - GI - EŠ

šu-u-lu[2] *lim-nu-tu*[3] *ša tub-ḳi it-ta-nam-za-zu šu-nu*

ZI AN-NA KAN-PA-NE-EŠ ZI KI-A KAN-PA-NE-EŠ

niš šame(*e*) *lu - u - ta - mu - u niš irṣitim*(*tim*) *lu - u - ta - mu - u*

INIM - INIM - MA SAG - GIG . . . .

EN DINGIR SAR(?) SAG-KAL ID-KAB-BU BA(?) . . DA PA . .

---

[1] 91,011 inserts A-MEŠ.

[2] 91,011, *šu-nu.*

[3] 91,011, *tum.*

In Eridu seven are they,
Seven are they, catching Ea in their toils,
From the Ocean they have come forth,
They are the evil cough (?)[a] which stands close by.
By Heaven may they be exorcised! By Earth may they be exorcised!

Prayer of the Sick Head.[b]

---

[a] *Šûlu* occurs in the list of diseases, *W.A.I.*, ii, 17, 25. Cf. the Syriac *š'ʿal* "to cough," *š'ʿûla* "a cough." The variant gives *šunu*, "they."

[b] No. 46,291, according to its colophon, was copied in the tenth year of Alexander, and No. 91,011 in the fourty-fourth year of . . .

The Sixth Tablet.

(PLATE XIV.)

. . . .

. . UŠ GIŠ - LIKIR . . . .

. . [*z*]*i - ka - ru lib - bi - š*[*u*] . . . .

. . . . NIM ERIN . . . .

. . . . *ik lil - li* . . . .

[ŠU]-SAR *III* - A - [AN] . . . [U-ME-NI-NU-NU]

[*pi*]-*kur - tu šu - uš* - [*lu - uš*] . . . [*ṭi-me-ma*]

[KA]-SAR *VII*-A-DU-[*II*-A-AN U-ME-NI-KEŠDA]

[*ki - ṣi*]*r si - bit a - di* [*ši-na ku-ṣur-ma*]

[NAM - ŠU]B NUN - KI - [GA U - ME - NI - SUM]

[*ši - p*]*at* ^{alu}[*Eridi i - di - ma*]

[SAG] MULU - TUR - RA - GE [U - ME - NI - KEŠDA]

[*ḳaḳ-ḳa*] - *da mar - ṣi* [*ru - ku - us - ma*]

[UTUG-Ḫ]UL A-LA-ḪUL BAR-[KU ḪE-IM-TA-GUB]

[*u-tuk*]-*ku lim-nu a-lu-u lim-nu ina a*-[*ḫa-ti li-iz-ziz*]

---

15. [UTUG] - * ŠIG-GA ALAD - * ŠIG-GA ḪE - EN - DA - [LAḪ - LAḪ - GI - EŠ]

[*še-e-du*] *dum-ḳi la-mas-si dum-ḳi i-da-a-šu* [*lu-u-ka-a-a-an*]

[INIM] - INIM - MA SAG - GIG - [GA - MEŠ]

[EN] . . . A NAM DI EN DA RI DA . . . .

Duppi VI KAM-ME SAG - GIG - MEŠ *Ekalli* m ilu *Aššur* - [*bani - apli*] . . .[1]

[Etc.]

[1] Lines 5–15 have been restored from Tablet IX of this series (ll. 230 ff., Pl. 24). They are exactly the same, and the reader is referred to Tablet IX (p. 64 ff.) for the translation and explanation.

Tablet "O."

Obverse.

(Plate XIV.)

EN SAG-GIG MUL-ANA-GIM AN-EDIN-NA NUN-KI-DA NU-UB-ZU

mu-ru-uṣ ḳaḳ-ḳa-di[1] *ki-ma kak-kab ša-ma-mi ina ṣi*[2]*-ri na-di-ma ul na-a-di*

SUR-AŠ-ŠUB IM-*SIG-*SIG-GA-GIM MULU-DIM-MA BA-AN-DU-DU

ṭi-'-u[3] *šur-bu-u*[4] *ki-ma ir-pi-te muk-kal-pi-te ana*[5] *bu-un-na-*[6]*ni e ameli*[7] *it-taš-kan*

AZAG TUR-RA NU-DUG-GA MULU IGI-NU-UN-BAR-RA

a-šak-ku mur-ṣu la ṭa-a-bu ša la nap-lu-si

MULU DINGIR NU-TUK-RA SILA-A-AN DU-A-NI-TA

la be-ili ilâni^{pl} *su-u-ku a-na a-la-ki-šu*

SAG-GIG TU-GIM BA-AN-DUL-DUL-LA

mu-ru-uṣ ḳaḳ-ḳa-di ki-ma ṣu-ba-ti ik-[*ta-tam-šu*]

SUR-AŠ-ŠUB SA-PAR-GIM . . . .

ti-'-u šu-ru-ub-bu [*u ki-ma sa-pa-ri*] . . . .

AZAG TUR-RA . . . .

a-šak-ku [*mur-ṣu*] . . . .

. . . .

[Reverse contains the remains of seven lines of the colophon.]

Tablet "O."

Obverse.

(Plate XIV.)

Incantation :—

Headache lieth like the stars of heaven in the desert and hath no praise [a]

Pain in the head and shivering like a scudding cloud turn unto the form of a man,

Fever, the evil disease which none can see ;

He that hath no gods—when he walketh in the street

Headache like a garment will envelop him,

The pain and shivering like a net will [entrap him]

Fever . . . .

. . . .

---

[1] 42,350, *du*.

[2] 42,350 inserts *e*.

[3] 42,350 omits.

[4] 42,350, *šu-ru-ub-bu-u*.

[5] 42,350, *a-na*.

[6] 42,350 inserts *an*.

[7] 42,350, *a-me-[li]*.

[a] *Nadi-ma ul nâdi*, probably intended as a play on words. The Sumerian may be translated "is not known."

The Eighth Tablet.

Obverse.

Col. I (Plate XV).

. . . .
. . . . NI (?) - BAR - BAR - RA
. . . . *mut - taḫ - ri - ir - ru*
. . . . MU - UN - LAḪ - LAḪ - GI - EŠ
. . . [*ina lib*?] - *bi a - lu it - ta - na - al - la - ḳu*
. . . . GAB - IM - MA - AN - RI - EŠ
. . . *zu* (?) - *mu - ur ilâni*^{pl} *im - taḫ - ḫa - ru - u*
[ID-BI]-TA BA-AN . . . . AN-BU-I-EŠ
a-na i-di-šu . . . . [*iš-du-du-u-ma*]
SU-NA IM-MI-I[N-] . . . . RI
zu-mur-šu im-ḫa-[*ṣu*] . . . . *-ta*
E - A - NI - KU IM - MA . . . . UŠ
a - na bi - ti - šu ir - [*ru - bu*] *- šu*
GIŠ - GI - EN - GIN - NA - BI BA - AN - BIR - BIR - [RI] - EŠ
bi - na - ti - šu u - sap - pi - [*i*]*ḫ*
DIMMU-BI BA-AN-KUR SU-NA BA-AN-DA-ḪA . . .
[*ṭe*] *- en - šu uš - tan - nu - u ši - ri - šu uš - tam - šu - u*
[MULU]-GIŠGAL-LU-BI : *a-me-lu šu-u mar-ṣi-iš i-na-kas* : A-GIG-GA I . . . .
DINGIR-SILIG-MULU-ŠAR IGI : GAR-GA-E : GIN-NA DU-MU
GIN-AZAG-GA : *ḳa-nu-u el-lu li-ḳi-e-ma* : ŠU-U-ME-TI
MULU-GIŠGAL-LU-BI : *a-me-lu* MU-*a-tim šum-di-id-ma* : U-ME-NI-DU-DU
GI-SAG-DU-SA-A : „ *- u bi-ni-ma* : U-ME-NI-DIM

The Eighth Tablet.

OBVERSE.

COL. I (PLATE XV).

. . . .
. . . . . . that dasheth in pieces,
They roam through the city . . . . . .
. . . unto the body (?) of the gods they approach,
Unto his side [they have drawn] . . . and
They have smitten his body . . . . . .
They have entered his house,
They have wasted his limbs,
They have driven him mad,
They have made him forget his flesh;
This man hath been grievously cut down.
Marduk hath seen him (etc.),
"What I" (etc.),
"Go, my son (Marduk),
"Take a clean reed and
"Measure that man and
"Make a reed hat (?) [a] and

---

[a] GI-SAG-DU-SA-A (or in l. 29 GI-SAG-DA-SA-U), of which we do not know the Assyrian equivalent. The meaning "hat" is suggested by the following three points: (1) the measuring of the man in l. 21, (2) the use of the character SAG, "head," in the ideogram, (3) the incantation being for a headache.

NAM-ŠUB NUN-KI-GA : *ši-pat* *aluEridi* *i-di-ma* : U-ME-NI-SUM

MULU-GIŠGAL-LU DU DINGIR-RA-NA : *a-me-lu ma-ri ili-šu ku-up-pir-ma* : U-ME-TE-GUR-GUR

MUḪ-BI U-ME-NI-ḪAS GAR-GA-SAG-IL-LA-BI-ḪE-A

e - li - šu ši - bir - ma lu - u di - na - nu - šu

UTUG-ḪUL A-LA-ḪUL BAR-KU ḪE-IM-TA-GUB

UTUG- * ŠIG-GA ALAD- * ŠIG-GA ḪE-EN-LAḪ-LAḪ-GI-EŠ

INIM-INIM-MA GI-SAG-DA-SA-U GAR-GA-SAG-GIL-LA-GE

EN UTUG - ḪUL - IK SAG - GIL (?) GUB - BA - BA

A-LA-ḪUL-IK SAG-GIL (?) GUB-BA-BA : GIDIM-ḪUL-IK „

MULLA-ḪUL-IK KI „ : DINGIR-ḪUL-IK KI „

MAŠKIM-ḪUL-IK KI „ : UTUG-DINGIR-LUGAL-KAN-ME ḪUL-IK KI „

MULU-GIŠGAL-LU PAP-ḪAL-LA SAG-GIG-GA-A-AN : MULU-GIŠGAL-LU-BI AZAG-GIG-GA-A-AN :

GIŠ - NAD - DA - A - NI BAR (?) - GA - A - AN

GIŠ-NA NAM-MULU-GIŠGAL-LU-GE ŠU NAM-TAR KA-A-NI ŠIB-BA NE-IN-SIG-GA :

[DINGIR-SILIG-MULU]-ŠAR IGI : GAR-GA-E : GIN-NA DU-MU

. . . . AZAG-GA NI-GIŠ-GIM NI-DUG-GA-GE

. . . . DINGIR-ŠE- * NAG-GE

. . . . [K]A-KA-SI-GE

. . . . NA-EN ID-DA-GE

. . . . RA-GE

. . . . GE

. . . .

" Perform the Incantation of Eridu and
" Make an 'atonement' for the man the son of his god and
" Upon him break (it) and let it be his substitute."
" That the evil Spirit, the evil Demon may stand aside,
" And a kindly Spirit, a kindly Guardian be present."

PRAYER OF THE REED HAT (?) AS SUBSTITUTE.

Incantation :—
The evil Spirit hath set a net,
The evil Demon hath set a net,
The evil Ghost hath set a net,
The evil Devil hath set a net,
The evil God hath set a net,
The evil Fiend hath set a net,
The evil Hag-demon hath set a net,
So that the wanderer hath fallen sick of headache,
So that this man hath fallen sick of fever,
His couch . . . . . (?)
On the couch of the man the Hand of Pestilence hath smitten his mouth.
Marduk hath seen (etc.),
" What I " (etc.),
" Go, my son (Marduk),
" [Take] . . . . a pure . . of oil, a . . of goodly oil,
" . . . . of Nisaba
" . . . .
" . . . . of the river
" . . . .

[Of Cols. II and V only the left halves remain ; Cols. III and IV are entirely lost.]

Col. II (Plate XVI).

(1) . . . . BA-U (?) . . . . . . (2) . . . . . SAG-GA . . . . . (3) ZI DINGIR-GIR-AN-NA-GE [KAN-PA], (4) ZI DINGIR-A-NUN-NA DINGIR-GAL-GAL-E-NE [KAN-PA], (5) MULU-GIŠGAL-LU-BI ḪE-EN-EL-LA [ḪE-EN-AZAG-GA ḪE-EN-LAḪ-LAḪ-GA], (6) ŠU-* ŠIG-GA DINGIR-RA-NA-KU ḪE-E[N-ŠI-IN-GE-GE]

(7) INIM - INIM - MA . . . .

(8) EN UTUG-ḪUL-IK MULU-RA IN . . . . . . (9) A-LA ḪUL-IK ŠU-IN-DIB . . . . (10) MULLA-ḪUL-IK MULU-RA KA . . . . (11) . . . . GIM IM-TA-SUM-MA : . . . . . (12) . . . BIL SAG-GIG-GA . . . . (13) . . . ḪUL-DE-NA . . . . . (14) MULU . . NA ŠUB-BA-A . . . . (15) MULU GAR (?) KU[E] . . . . . (16) MULU A NAK-E . . . . . (17) MULU GIŠ-ŠA-KA-NA-GE . . . . (18) MULU GIN SIL-A-TA . . . . . . (19) MULU DINGIR-GUD IR-TA . . . . (20) MULU-ID-GUD ZI-GA-TA . . . . . (21) MULU KI-TUŠ-BI-TA . . . . . (22) MULU KI-NA-BI-TA . . . . . . (23) GUD-TUR-RA . . . . (24) LU AMAŠ . . . . (25) SUK-RA ḪA ḪU-NA . . . (26) * BIR-ANŠU GAR UR * TATTAB-BA EDIN-NA . . . . (27) UTUG EDIN-NA UTUG ḪAR-SAG . . . (28) UTUG A-RI-A UTUG ID-DA . . . (29) UTUG GIŠ-ŠAR UTUG SILA-A . . . . . (30) MAŠKIM EDIN-NA UTUG-ḪUL-IK-E . . . (31) MULU-MULU GAN (?) KA-GA . . . (32) MULU NAM-NE-ŠUB-BA KUD-DA . . . (33) MULU-GIŠGAL-LU DU DINGIR-RA-NA SAG-GA . . . (34) UTUG-ḪUL IK-E SU-NI . . . . (35) ALAD * ŠIG-GA AN-NA . . . . (36) ALAD ALAD E-A-ZU . . . . (37) TU-* ŠIG-GA NAM-TIL-LA . . . (38) ID-ZI-DA ID-KAB-BU . . . (39) . . . SI LA . . . (40) [K]U-SUR-RA.

[Cols. III and IV are entirely broken away.]

REVERSE.

COL. V (PLATE XVII).

(1) . . . . . . (2) KU . . . (3) DINGIR . . . (4) . . . . . . (5) . . . . NE . . . . (6) . . . . U NA . . . . (7) GIŠ-ḪAR GIŠ-MA-NU . . . (8) BI (?) GAR . . . A . . . (9) NAM-ŠUB NUN-KI-GA . . . . . (10) MULU GIŠGAL-LU DU DINGIR-RA-[NA] . . . . . . (11) MUḪ-NA NIGIN (?)-NA . . . . . . (12) UTUG-ḪUL A-LA-ḪUL BAR-KU [ḪE-IM-TA-GUB] (13) UTUG-*ŠIG-GA ALAD-*ŠIG-GA [ḪE-EN-LAḪ-LAḪ-GI-EŠ]

(14) INIM - INIM - MA DUG . . . .

(15) EN . . GIŠ-ŠAR-TA GA TA . . . (16) . . DINGIR-EN-KI-GE GIL (?) GIŠ-ŠAR-TA . . . (17) GIŠ-ŠAR MA-DA (?) BI . . . UN . . . (18) GA IL-LA-A-AN . . . (19) ŠI-TA . . . LA A . . . (20) DU-NI DINGIR-SILIG-[MULU-ŠAR] . . . MU-UN . . . (21) GIN-NA DU-MU DINGIR-SILIG-[MULU-ŠAR] . . . (22) GIŠ . . . SAR . . . NE . . . (23) KA-LUM-MA-NI GIŠ-GIŠIMMAR . . . (24) MULU-GIŠGAL-LU DU DINGIR-RA-NA NAM . . . . (25) *VII*-A-DU *II*-NA ŠU-SAR . . (26) KA-SAR [U-ME-NI-KEŠDA] (27) NAM-NE-ŠUB TAR-RÙ-DA-BI . . . (28) NAM-NE-ŠUB MU (?) DINGIR-RA . . . (29) NAM-NE-ŠUB KA-LUM-MA . . . . (30) ŠU-SAR-GIM ḪE-EN-BUR . . . . (31) EME-ḪUL-LU-IK BAR-KU [ḪE-IM-TA-GUB]

(32) INIM - INIM - MA GIŠ . . . .

EN NA NE KUR - TA A - RI . . . .
KA (?) . . . .
. . . .

COL. VI (PLATE XVIII).

. . . .
. . . . ZI DA
. . . . *da - ' - i - ku*
. . . . GU - MU - UN - NA - AN - DE - E
. . . . *beli al - si*
. . . GA . . . GU - MU - UN - NA - AN - DE - E
. . . . . . *- lum* *ilu Ea ša* . . . . . *al - si*
[GIŠ]-MA-NU GIŠ-KU-MAḪ AN-NA-GE ŠU-U-ME-TI
e-ra (?) *kak-ku ṣi-i-ri ša ilu A-nim li-ḳi-ma*
UR - PA - BI BIL U - NE - TAG
ap - pi u iš - di i - ša - a - tum lu - up - [pit] - ma
NAM - ŠUB NUN - KI - GA U - ME - NI - SUM
ši - pat alu Eridi i - di - ma
SAG MULU - TUR - RA - GE U - ME - NI - GAR
ina ri - eš mar - ṣa šu - kun - ma
UTUG - ḪUL A - LA - ḪUL BAR - KU ḪE - IM - TA - GUB
UTUG- * ŠIG-GA ALAD- * ŠIG-GA ḪE-EN-LAḪ-LAḪ-GI-EŠ

EN SAG-GIG AN-EDIN-NA NI-DU-DU IMI-GIM MU-UN-RI-RI

IM - DUB *XXIV* SAR NAM NAR KU - KAR
UTUG - ḪUL - MEŠ NU - AL - BAD

COL. VI (PLATE XVIII).

. . . .

. . . . slaying.

. . . . I call,

. . . . of Ea . . . . I call,

"Take the tamarisk, the potent weapon of Anu,

10. "Set it alight in front and behind,

"Perform the Incantation of Eridu and

15. "Put it on the head of the sick man,

"That the evil Spirit, the evil Devil may stand aside,

"And a kindly Spirit, a kindly Guardian be present."

Incantation: "Headache roameth in the desert, blowing like the wind."

TWENTY-FOURTH TABLET WRITTEN . . . (?) SERIES "EVIL SPIRITS" INCOMPLETE.[a]

---

[a] The colophon states that the tablet was written in the 129th year (of the Seleucid era), i.e. 183 B.C.

The Ninth Tablet.

Obverse.

Col. I (Plate XIX).

EN SAG-GIG AN-NA-EDIN-NA NI-DU-DU IMI-GIM MU-UN-RI-RI

mu-ru-uṣ ḳaḳ-ḳa-di ina ṣi-e-ri it-tak-kip ki-ma ša-a-ri i-zaḳ[1]*-ḳa*

NIM-GIR-GIM MU-UN-GIR-GIR-RI SIG-NIM NE-IN-ŠU-ŠU

ki-ma bir-ḳi it-ta-nab-riḳ e-liš u šap-liš it-ta-na-at-bak

IM-NU-TEMEN-NA DINGIR-RA-NA GI-GIM IN-ŠA-ŠA

la pa-li-iḫ ili-šu ki-ma ḳa-ni-e iḫ-ta-aṣ-ṣi-iṣ[2]

SA-BI GI-ḪA-AN-GIM AN-SIL-SIL-LA

bu-a-ni-šu ki-ma [kanu]*ḫi-ni u-šal-liṭ*

AMA-DINGIR-NINNI LI-TAR NU-TUK-A UZU-BI IN-SIG-SIG-GA

ša [ilu]*Iš-tar pa-ḳi-da la i-šu-u šîri*[pl]*-šu u-šaḫ-ḫa-aḫ*

MUL-ANA-GIM SUR-SUR-RA A-GIM GIG-A AL-GIN-GIN

ki-ma kak-kab ša-ma-me i-ṣar-ru-ur ki-ma mê[pl] *mu-ši il-lak*

MULU-GIŠGAL-LU PAP-ḪAL-LA GAB-RI-A-NI BA-AN-GAR U-GIM MU-UN-DA-RU-UŠ

ana a-me-li mut-tal-li-ki me-iḫ-ri iš-ša-kin-ma ki-ma ûme(me) iḫ-me-šu

MULU-GIŠGAL-LU-BI BA-AN-GAZ-EŠ

a-me-li šu-a-tu i-duk-ma

The Ninth Tablet.

OBVERSE.

COL. I (PLATE XIX).

Incantation :—

Headache roameth over the desert, blowing like the wind,
Flashing like lightning, it is loosed above and below ;
It cutteth off him who feareth not his god like a reed,
Like a stalk of henna[a] it slitteth his thews.
It wasteth the flesh of him who hath no protecting goddess,
Flashing like a heavenly star, it cometh like the dew ;
It standeth hostile against the wayfarer, scorching him like the day,
This man it hath struck and

---

[1] K. 5,287, *za*.

[2] K. 5,287, *ṣi*.

[a] *Ḫinu*, also written *ḫinnu* (Tablet "P," l. 31), is probably to be referred to the Arabic word حِنَّاء, "henna." It occurs also in both forms without the determinative GI in the late Babylonian contracts, which would point to the produce of the henna-plant being used in Babylonia as a marketable commodity. (Strassmaier, *Nabonidus*, 234, 12, etc.)

MULU-GIŠGAL-LU-BI ŠA-DIB-BA-GIM ŠU-TA-TA-GUR-GUR-RA

a-me-lu šu-u ki-ma ša ki-iṣ lib-bi it-ta-nak-ra-ru

ŠA - ZI - GA - GIM IN - BAL - BAL - E

ki-ma[1] *ša lib-ba-šu na-as-ḫu it-ta-nab-lak-kat*

BIL ŠUB - BU - DA - GIM IN - TAB - TAB - E

ki-ma ša ina i-ša-ti na-du-u iḫ-tam-maṭ

ANŠU-EDIN-NA KAS-KAS-DA-GIM IGI-NA IM-DIR AN-SI

ki-ma pu-ri-me[2] *ša ḫa-am-ra êni*$^{II\,pl}$*-šu u-pi-e ma-la-a*

ZI - NI - TA UR[3] - IN - DA - AN - KU - KU KI - NAM - BAD BA - AN - KEŠDA

it-ti na-piš-ti-šu i-tak-kal it-ti mu-u-ti ra-kis

SAG-GIG IM-DUGUD-DUGUD-DA-GIM A-GUB-BI MULU-NA-ME NU-UN-ZU

ṭi-'-u[3] *ša ki-ma im-ba-ri kab-tu a-lak-ta-šu man-ma ul i-di*

ŠI + UM[4] -TIL-LA-BI KA-SAR-BI MULU-NA-ME NU-UN-ZU

it-ta-šu ga-mir-tu mar-ka-as-su man-ma ul i-di

DINGIR-SILIG-MULU-ŠAR IGI : GAR-GA-E : GIN-NA DU-MU

U-ḪUL-TI-GIL-LA DINGIR-EDIN-NA AŠ-NA SAR-A

„ *- a ša ina ṣi - e - ri e - diš - ši - šu a - ṣu - u*

DINGIR-BABBAR E-A-NA[5] TUR-RA-NA-KU SAG-ZU U-ME-NI-DUL

ki-ma ^{ilu}*Ša-maš a-na bi-ti-šu e-ri-bi ṣu-ba-ta ḳaḳ-ḳad-ka kut-tim-ma*

U-ḪUL-TI-GIL-LA U-ME-NI-DUL ZID U-ME-NI-ḪAR

„ *- a kut - tim - ma ḳi - ma e - ṣir - ma*

ID-TIG-ZI-GA-TA DINGIR-BABBAR NAM-TA-E

ina še - e - ri ḷa - am ^{ilu}*Šamši a - ṣi - e*

Like one with heart disease he staggereth,
Like one bereft of reason he is broken,
Like that which hath been cast into the fire he is shrivelled,
Like a wild ass . . . . his eyes are full of cloud,
On himself he feedeth, bound in death;
Headache whose course like the dread windstorm none knoweth,
None knoweth its full time or its bond.
Marduk hath seen him: (etc.),
" What I "; (etc.),
" Go, my son (Marduk),
" The wild cucumber (?) which springeth up by itself in the desert,
" When the Sun entereth his dwelling
" Cover thy head with a cloth and
" Cover the cucumber (?) and surround it with meal and
" In the morning before the Sun riseth,

---

[1] K. 4,865, *i*.
[2] K. 4,865, *mi*.
[3] K. 4,865 omits.
[4] K. 4,865 inserts BI.
[5] K. 4,865, AN.

KI-GUB-BA[1] -A-NI-TA : *ina man-za-zi-[šu u]-suḫ-šu-ma* : U-ME-NI-SIR

?-BI : *su[2]-ru-us-[su li-ḳi-e]-ma* : ŠU-U-ME-TI

SIG-RIK-KAR UŠ-NU-ZU ŠU-U-ME-TI

ša-rat u-ni-ki la [pi]-ti-ti li-ḳi-e-ma

(PLATE XX.)

SAG MULU-TUR-RA-GE[3] U-ME-NI-KEŠDA

ḳaḳ-ḳa-di mar-ṣi[4] ru-ku-us-ma

TIG MULU-TUR-RA-GE : *ki-šad mar-[ṣi] ru-kus-ma* : U-ME-NI-KEŠDA

SAG-GIG SU MULU-GIŠGAL-LU-GE . . . A-GIM[5] ḪE-IM-MA-RA-AN-ZI-ZI

mu-ru-uṣ ḳaḳ-ḳa-di ša ina zumur [a]-me-li[6] ba-šu-u li-in-na-si-iḫ

IN-NU-RI IM-RI-A-GIM KI-BI-KU N'A-AN-GA-GA

ki-ma il-ti ša ša-a-ru ub-lu-ši ana aš-ri-šu a-a i-tur

ZI AN-NA KAN-PA ZI KI-A KAN-PA

EN SAG-GIG ḪAR-SAG-GIM BUL-DA NU-UB-ZU-A

mu-[ru]-uṣ ḳaḳ-ḳa-di ša ki-ma šade(e)[7] ana nu-uš-šu[8] la na-ṭu-u

[SAG-GIG] IM-DIR *DIRIG-GA-GIM MULU-RA MU-UN-NA-TE

[mu-ru-uṣ] ḳaḳ-ḳa-di ki-ma ir-pi-ti muk-kal-pi-ti[9] ana ameli iṭ-ḫi

[SUR-AŠ-ŠUB ?] IMI-GIM E-NE-RA MU . . . .

[ṭi'u ? šu]-ru-ub-bu-u ki-ma ša-a-ri ana šu-a-ti . . .

. . . . ID-ŠU-GIR-BI SA AD NIM IN (?) . . .

. . . . *meš-ri-ti-šu ša-aš-ša-ṭu* . . . . . .

[Hiatus of about three lines.]

"Tear it up from its place
"And take its root;
"Take the hair of a virgin kid

(PLATE XX.)

"And bind it on the head of the sick man,
"And bind it on the neck of the sick man,
"That the Headache which is in the body of this man may be carried away
"And may not return to its place,
"Like the straw which the wind whirleth away!"
By Heaven be thou exorcised! By Earth be thou exorcised!

Incantation:—
Headache, which like a mountain cannot be moved,
Headache like a scudding cloud hath attacked the man,
[Pain in the head], shivering, like a wind [hath rushed on] this man
. . . . his limbs sores (?) . . . . .

[Hiatus of about three lines.]

---

[1] K. 5,141 omits.
[2] K. 5,141, *šu*.
[3] K. 5,141, GIG-GA-NA-GE for MULU-TUR-RA-GE.
[4] K. 5,141, *kaḳ-ḳad* . . . . for *kaḳ-ḳa-di mar-ṣi*.
[5] K. 5,141 . . . NI-IK for A-GIM.
[6] K. 5,141, *ameli*.
[7] K. 5,141, *i* for *e*.
[8] K. 5,141, *ši*.
[9] K. 3,169, *te*.

. . . . *ul i - šat* (?) *- ti*
. . . DUG - GA . . . . DA - KU - KU
[*šut* ?]*-ta ṭa-ab-*[*ta* . . . . . . *ul*] *i-ṣal-lal*
[ID-ŠU]-GIR-BI : *meš-ri-ti-*[*šu ul u-tir* : MU]-UN-
DA-AN-GE-GE
[ID-ŠU]-GIR-BI NU-MU-UN-DA-AN-[IL-LA : *meš-ri-ti*]*-šu*
ul i-na-aš-ši
[GIŠ]-GI-EN-GI-BI . . . . RI (?)
bi-na-ti-šu a-ḫi . . . . *-an*
[U]-GUG-GIM BA-AN-NA . . . KU ḪE . . . .
[*ki*]*-ma ur-ba-ti ni-il* . . . . *su ik* . . .

Col. II.

'U-A A-A : *ina* „ „ *ûme*(*me*)*-šam uš-ta-bar-ri* :
U-ME-NI-IB[1]-ZAL-ZAL-E
DINGIR-SILIG-MULU-ŠAR : GAR-GA-E : GIN-NA DU-MU
SIG-RIK-KAR UŠ-NU-ZU : *ša-rat u-ni-ki la pi-ti-ti li-ḳi-ma* :
ŠU-U-ME-TI
SAL MUD-DA-GA-A ID-ZI-DA-KU U-ME-NI-SAR
ID-KAB-BU-KU U-ME-NI-TAB
sin-niš-tu pa-ris-tu im-na liṭ-me-ma šu-me-la li-ṣip
KA - SAR *VII* A - DU - *II* - A - AN U - ME - NI - SAR
ki - ṣir si - bit a - di ši - na ku - ṣur - ma
NAM-ŠUB ERI-DUG-GA[2]: *ši-pat* ^{alu}*Eridi i-di-ma* :
U-ME-NI-SUM
SAG MULU-TUR-RA-GE : *ḳaḳ-ḳad mar-ṣi ru-kus-ma* :
U-ME-NI-KEŠDA

(Plate XXI.)

TIG MULU-TUR-RA-GE : *ki-šad mar-ṣi ru-kus-ma* :
U-ME-NI-KEŠDA
ZI - PA - RAM - NA - GE : *na - piš - ta - šu ru - kus - ma* :
U - ME - NI - KEŠDA
ID - ŠU - GIR - BI : *meš - ri - ti - šu ruk - kis - ma* :
U - ME - NI - KEŠDA - KEŠDA

. . . . he cannot drink,
With pleasant dreams (?) he sleepeth not,
His limbs he cannot move,
His limbs he cannot raise,
His limbs [appear ?] strange (?)
Like a reed [a] he bendeth . . . .

Col. II.

Each day with cries of woe he is sated.
Marduk hath seen him : (etc.),
" What I " ; (etc.),
" Go, my son (Marduk),
" Take the hair of a virgin kid,
" Let a wise woman spin (it) on the right side
" And double it on the left,[b]
" Bind knots twice seven times,
" And perform the Incantation of Eridu,
" And bind the head of the sick man,

(Plate XXI.)

" And bind the neck of the sick man,
" And bind the soul [c] of the sick man,
" And bind up his limbs,

---

[1] K. 5,141, UD-MI-NI-IB . . . for U-ME-NI-IB-ZAL-ZAL-E.

[2] K. 5,141, NUN-KI-GA for ERI-DUG-GA.

[a] *Urbatu*, cf. Syr. *arbhânâ*, Brockelmann, *Lexicon*, p. 25*b*.

[b] Among certain savage tribes it is often the custom to spin a thread by rolling the strands sharply along the right thigh with the hand, and it seems that some such process is suggested here. (See Tylor, *Anthropology*, p. 246.)

[c] Fossey, *La Magie Assyrienne* (Paris, 1902), p. 466, suggests "*peut-être . . . un euphémisme pour désigner le membre viril.*" On the other hand, "to bind the soul" would be quite intelligible in modern savage witchcraft. (See Fraser, *Golden Bough*, vol. i, p. 247.)

GIŠ - * NAD - DA - NA - GE U - ME - NI - NIGIN - E

ir - ša - šu li - me - ma

A NAM - ŠUB MUḪ - NA U - ME - NI - SUM

mê^pl^ šip - ti e - li - šu i - di - ma

SAG-GIG I-NE-IM-GUB-BA-GIM AN-NA ḪA-BA-GIBIŠ-NE

mu-ru-uṣ ḳaḳ-ḳa-di ki-ma ḳut-ri ma-zal-ti ni-iḫ-ti ana šame(e) li-til-la

A - TAK - BAL - E - NE KI - KU ḪA - BA - GIBIŠ - NE

ki-ma [me]-e ri-[ḫi-ti] tab-ku-ti ana irṣitim(tim) li-rid

I DINGIR - EN - KI - GE PA - HE[1] - E - A - GE

a - mat ^ilu^ E - a liš - te - pi

DINGIR - DAM - GAL - NUN - NA SI - ḪE - EN - SI - DI - E

^ilu^ Dam - ki - na liš - te - šir

DINGIR-SILIG-? NUN-NA DU-SAG ZU-AB-GE * ŠAG-GA TAG-TAG-LI-BI ZA-A-KAN[2]

^ilu^ Marduk. mâr riš-tu-u ša ap-si-i bu-un-[nu] u du-um-mu-ḳu ku-um-ma[3]

EN SAG - GIG MULU - RA . . MU - UN - GA - GA

mu-ru-uṣ ḳaḳ-ḳa-di a-na a-[me]-li iš-ša-kin-ma

SAG-GIG GU-SA-A GIG MULU . . . MU-UN-GA-GA

ṭi-'-u mu-ru-uṣ da-ad-da-[ni a]-me-lu iš-ša-kin-ma

SAG - GIG A - MI - A - GIM IN - DU - DU - NE

mu-ru-uṣ ḳaḳ-ḳa-di ki-ma [a]-gi-e it-tak-kip

SAG-GIG DINGIR-BABBAR-E-TA . . KU (?) DINGIR-BABBAR-ŠU-A-KU

mu-ru-uṣ ḳaḳ-ḳa-di iš-tu ṣi-[it ^ilu^] Šamši(ši) ana e-rib ^ilu^ Šamši(ši)

SAG - GIG ḪAR - GUB GU - MU - UN - NA - AN - DE - E

mu-ru-uṣ ḳaḳ-ḳa-di i-ra-mu-um i-ša-as-si

"And surround his couch,

"And cast the water of the Incantation over him,

"That the Headache may ascend to heaven like the smoke from a peaceful homestead,

"That like water-lees poured out it may go down into the earth.

"May the Word of Ėa make clear,

"May Damkina direct aright.

"O Marduk, eldest son of the Deep! Thine is the power to brighten and bless!"

Incantation:—

Headache hath settled upon the man and

Sickness of the head, the disease of woe (?) hath settled upon the man.

Headache like a flood roameth loose,

Headache from Sunrise to Sunset,

Headache shrieketh and crieth.

---

[1] K. 5,213 apparently omits.

[2] K. 5,213, GE.

[3] K. 5,213, *-mu* TU-EN after *um*.

A-AB-BA : *ina tamtim(tim) ir-ṣi-ti rapašti(ti)* :
KI-GAR-DAGAL-LA-A-KU
A - MI - A DU - DU - LA A - MI - A IN - GUB
a - gi - i ṣi - iḫ - ḫi - ru - ti a - gi - e il - lak
A-MI-A GAL-GAL-LA : *a-gu-u rab-bu-ti a-gu-šu* : A-MI-A-BI
AN BUR-NUN-SI-A : *rap-ša uz-ni mâr* ^{alu}*Eridi* : DU
NUN-KI-GA-GE
SAG - GIG GUD - GIM IN - DU - DU - E - NE
mu-ru-uṣ ḳaḳ-ḳad kima al-pi it-tak-kip
SAG - GIG LIKIR - GA - GIM IN - DU - DU - NE
mu-ru-uṣ ḳaḳ-ḳa-di ki-ma ki-iṣ lib-bi it-ta-kip
A-A-NI-IR BA-AN-TE LI-TAR BA-NI-IB-GE-GE
a - na a - bi - šu iṭ - ḫi - e - ma [ip -]ta - na - al - šu

(Plate XXII.)

A - A - MU SAG - GIG MULU - RA ŠA - MU - UN - GA - GA
a-bi m[u-ru-u]ṣ ḳaḳ-ḳa-di ana a-me-li iš-ša-kin-ma
INGAR-[GIM . . .]-AN-BU-EŠ MUḪ-NA BA-AN-ŠUB
ki-ma [igari ša li]-bit-ta-šu šal-pat e-li-šu it-ta-[di]
GIŠ . . . . ŠUB TUR-RA-BI MU-UN-SIG
. . . . *mu-ru-us-su lu-uk-kis*
. . . . MU-UN-NA-NI-IB-GE-GE
^{ilu}*E - a ši - tul - ta ip - pal - šu*
[GIN]-NA DU-MU GAR-ME-GAR SAG-GIG ḪU-LAḪ-ḪA-BI
a-lik ma-a-ri ḳu-u-lu mu-ru-uṣ ḳaḳ-ḳa-[di] šug-lit-ma
. . . ŠE-ŠIŠ : *ar-su-up-pu še-gu-šu in-nin-nu* :
ŠE-IN-NU-ḪA
[AB] - SIN - BI U DI - DUG - GA - BI
ša i - na ši - ir - ' - i - ša ûm(um) - ša kaš - da - at
UM - MA ŠU - EL - TA U - ME - NI - IB - ḪAR - ḪAR
pur-šum-tu ina ḳatâ$^{II\ pl}$*-ša ellâti*^{pl} *li-te-en-ma*

Through the Sea—the Broad Earth—
The Little Floods—(its) flood goeth,
Its flood is (as) the Mighty Floods.
O thou Wise Son of Eridu!
Headache steer-like roameth loose,
Headache like heart disease roameth loose!
Unto his father he drew nigh and answered him:

(PLATE XXII.)

" O father, Headache hath settled upon the man,
" It hath fallen upon him like a house wall
" Whereof the bricks have broken out;
" . . . that I may cut off his disease."
Ea his decision gave in answer to him:
" Go, O my son! Frighten the snare of Headache.
" The parsnip (?),[a] *šeguśu*-corn, *inninnu*-corn,[b]
" Which in its growth hath reached its day,
" Let an old woman bray it with clean hands;

---

[a] *Arsuppu*, possibly the Syriac *ḫûrs'phâ* (*v. ḫûrph'sâ*), *Raucus carota* (Brockelmann, 124*b*).

[b] On *inninnu* see Zimmern, *Bab. R.l.*, 41–42, I, 26.

UR-BI U-ME-NI-SAR-SAR GAR-LAG-GA U-ME-NI-SID
ištenîš(nîš) bu - lul - ma [lu ?] - uš - ma
SAG-GA-NA U-ME-NI-GAR : *ina ḳaḳ-ḳa-di-šu šu-kun ul-lil-šu-ma* : NA U-ME-NI-DAL
. . . . UB - BI EGIR - BI U - ME - NI - ŠUB
ša ina iz (?)-zu (?)-tu ḫu . . . ar-ki-šu u-suk-ma
SAG - GIG TU - ḪU - [GIM] AB - LAL - KU
mu-ru-uṣ ḳaḳ-ḳa-di [ki-ma su]-um-ma-ti ana ap-ti
NAM - ṢAB - ḪU - GIM [ANA] - BAL - KU
ki - ma a - ri - bi [a - na] . . . . šame(e)

COL. III.

ḪU-GIM KI-DAGAL-LA-KU ḪA-BA-NI-IB-DAL . . .
ki - ma iṣ - ṣu - ri aš - ri rap - ši lit - tap - ra - aš
ŠU- * ŠAG-GA DINGIR-RA-NA-KU ḪE-EN-ŠI-IN-GE-GE
a - na ḳatâ^{II} *damḳâti*^{pl} *ša ili - šu lip - pa - ḳid*

EN SAG-GIG ANA-TA-NA MU-UN-SAR-KI-A PA-ḪE-MU-UN-DA-AB-ZI
ṭi-'-u ina šame(e) ra-kis ina irṣitim(tim)[1] *in-na-as-sa-aḫ*
ŠUL ID - TUK ID - NA MU - UN - DA[2] - TIL
ša id-li be-el e-mu-ḳi e-mu-ḳi-šu uḳ-ta-at-ti
KI-EL * ŠIG-GA ID-NA NU-MU-UN-ŠI-IN-GE-GE
ša ar-da-ti da-me-iḳ-ti is-sa ul u-ta-ra
MULU - TUR - RA SU - NA MI - NI - IN - GAR - RI - EŠ
ša ina zu - um - ri mar - ṣi iš - šak - nu
DINGIR-NINNI E-ḪI-LI-A-TA NAM-A-A-TA NAM-AN-NA MULU-NU-TIL-LA-KU
KUR - TA IM - TA - E
^{ilu}*Iš-tar ša ina nu-uḫ-ḫi ul-ṣi ul-la-nu-uš-ša ma-am-man la i-ba-šu-u iš-tu šadi(i)*[3] *u-še-ri-da*

" Then mix it together and knead it,
" And put it on his head; wash him
" And place that which . . . behind him,
" That the Headache, like the dove to the cote,
" Like the raven to heaven,

COL. III.

" Like the bird of the open steppes, may fly away.
" Into the favouring hands of his god may he be commended."

Incantation :—

Headache, though bound in heaven, hath escaped on earth;
It bringeth to nought the strength of the hero, mighty in power,
It giveth not back the strength of the fair maid,
It hath settled on the body of the sick man;
Ishtar, besides whom there is none to give rest and happiness,
Hath let it come down from the mountains,

---

[1] K. 12,000, cc inserts *li*.
[2] K. 12,000, cc inserts AB.
[3] K. 12,000, cc . . . . *a-ti*.

(PLATE XXIII.)

GIŠ-GI-EN-GIN-NA MULU-GIŠGAL-LU PAP-ḪAL-LA MU-UN-NA-TE-EŠ
a-na bi-na-at a-me-li mut-tal-li-ki iṭ-ḫi-e-ma
SAG-GA 'U-A : *a-me-lu u-a e-te-mid* : BA-NI-IN-UŠ
A-BA ZI-ZI : *man-nu i-na-as-saḫ man-nu u-šat-ba* : A-BA-ZI-GI EŠ
DINGIR NANNA(NA) : ^{ilu}*Iš-tar ma-rat* ^{ilu}*Sin* : DU DINGIR-EN-ZU-NA-GE
DINGIR-EN-KUR-*SIG-NUN-ME-UBARA : ^{ilu} „ *mar* ^{ilu}*Bêli* : DU DINGIR-EN-LIL-LA-GE
DINGIR-SILIG-MULU-ŠAR : ^{ilu}*Marduk mar* ^{alu}*Eridi* : DU NUN-KI-[GA]
SU MULU-GIŠGAL-LU PAP-ḪAL-LA-GE ḪE-IB-TA-AN-ZI-ZI
zu-um-ri a-me-li mut-tal-li-ki li-šat-bu-u
DINGIR . . . . TE BAR-RA U-? . . . [SAG]-GA-NA BA-AN-KEŠDA
. . . . *ti*(?) *a-bi ša par-ṣa ri-ṣa-tum* [*ina*] *ḳaḳ-ḳad-su ir-ḳu-uṣ*
NI-[NUN-NA] TUR-AZAG-GA-TA MU-UN-TUM-MA
ḫi-me-ta ša iš-tu tar-ba-ṣi el-lu ub-lu-ni
GA AMAŠ-AZAG-GA-TA MU-UN-TUM-MA
ši-iz-bu ša iš-tu su-pu-ri el-lu ub-lu-u-ni
NI-NUN AZAG-GA TUR-EL-TA INIM-INIM-MA U-ME-NI-SUM
ana ḫi-me-ti ellitim(tim) ša tar-ba-ṣi el-lu šip-ta i-di-ma
MULU-GIŠGAL-LU DU DINGIR-RA-NA MU-UN-TAG-TAG
a-me-lu mâr ili-šu lu-up-pit-ma
MULU-GIŠGAL-LU-BI NI-NUN-NA-GIM ḪE-EN-AZAG-GA
a-me-lu šu-u ki-ma ḫi-me-ti li-lil

(PLATE XXIII.)

Unto the limbs of the wayfarer it hath drawn nigh, and
The man standeth in woe.
Who will remove it, who will drive it away?
Ishtar, daughter of Sin ——
Sin (?), son of Bel ——
Marduk, son of Eridu ——
From the body of the wayfarer they shall drive it away.
. . . . hath bound his head
Butter which they have brought from a clean fold,
Milk which they have brought from a clean stall;
With the pure butter from the clean fold perform the incantation,
And rub (it) on the man, the son of his god,
That that man may be pure like the butter,

GA - BI - GIM ḪE - EN - EL - LA
ki - ma ši - iz - bi šu - a - tu li - tab - bi - ib
KUBABBAR- * ŠIG-GIM MU-SIR-BI ḪU-UM-TA-LAḪ
ki-ma ṣar-pi ṣur-ru-pi ru-uš-šu-šu lit-tan-biṭ
ZABAR - GIM IM - SU - UB - TA ḪE - EN - TA - SU - UB
ki - ma ḳi - e maš - ši lim - ma - sis
DINGIR-BABBAR SAG-KAL DINGIR-RI-E-NE-GE SU-NA U-ME-NI-SUM
a-na ^{ilu}*Šamši a-ša-rid ilâni*^{pl} *pi-ḳid-su-ma*
DINGIR-BABBAR SAG-[KAL] DINGIR-RI-E-NE-GE SILIM-MA-NA ŠU * ŠAG-GA DINGIR-RA-NA-KU ḪE - EN - ŠI - IN - GE - GE
^{ilu}*Šamšu a-ša-rid ilâni*^{pl} *šal-mu-su ana ḳatâ*^{II} *damḳâti*^{pl} *ša ili-šu*
lip - ḳid - su EN

EN SAG-KI DIB-BA ḪAR-SAG-GA MULU-NU-UB-DA NU-UB-ZU
SUR-AŠ-SUB MULU-GIŠGAL LU-GIM BA-AN-DUL-DUL
MULU-DINGIR-NU-TUK-RA SILA-A GIN SI-DI-E
ALAM SILA-A ŠU UL KEŠDA(DA) NU-KEŠDA(DA)
ṢIR - A - GIM ṢIR - A - GIM ṢIR SAG SAR AŠ - A - AN
U NU - KU - KU GIG NU - KU - KU
DINGIR-SILIG-MULU-ŠAR IGI-IM-MA-AN-SUM : GAR-GA-E ṢA-A-MU : GIN-NA DU-MU
(PLATE XXIV.)
U - TAR - SIR U - ŠI - ŠI U - ŠI - MAN U - A - RIG(?)

---

[a] The ^{sammu}TAR-ṢIR (? "snake-bane") is mentioned on K. 4,152 (*Cun. Texts*, xiv, pl. 44, I–II, 11), *ina* ,, (= *ni-siḫ-tu*) BIR^{pl} ,, (= *ša tar-bul-lu*); the ^{sammu}ŠI-ŠI is explained by ^{sammu}*a-ši-i* (ibid., pl. 29, K. 4,566, I–II, 6), and there is a ^{sammu}ŠI-ŠI *ša iḳli*, as well as a ^{sammu}ŠI-MAN *ša iḳli* (ibid., pl. 43, K. 4,419, II, 8, 9).

180. That he may be clean like the milk,
That his skin (?) may shine like silver refined,
185. That he may be bright like shining copper.
Unto Shamash, Chieftain of the gods, commend him,
190. That Shamash, Chieftain of the gods, may commend
His welfare unto the kindly hands of his god.
Incantation.

Incantation :—
Disease of the temples (?) hath fallen on the man unknown in the mountains,
Shivering hath covered the man like a garment,
The man that hath no god when he walketh in the street
195. It taketh his shape in the street and none can bind it.
Like a snake, like a snake, a snake it bindeth the head,
So that he cannot rest by day or night.
Marduk hath seen, (etc.): "What I" (etc.): "Go, my son (Marduk),

(PLATE XXIV.)

"The plants TAR-ṢIR, ŠI-ŠI, ŠI-MAN, A . . . .[a]

---

^{sammu} ḪAR-ḪAR = ^{sammu} *ḫaltappânu* (pl. 20, II–III, 7) and ^{sammu} *karan šelibi*, "fox-grape" (pl. 22, VII–VIII, 52). ^{sammu} GUR-UŠ = *A-sar-ma du* (pl. 22, VII–VIII, 49). The ŠI-ŠI (?) plant is described as one of nine ^{sammu} ŠA-GIG (? plants with "dark hearts"), pl. 48, Rm. 328, rev. II, 6 ff. ^{sammu} KUR-KUR = ^{sammu} MAS-TAB-BA-RI-RI (a plant with a double . . .), pl. 29, K. 4,566, I–II, 31.

6

U - MULU - GIŠGAL - LU U - ḪAR - ḪAR U - KUR - KUR
KUL U - * GURU - UŠ RIG AN - BAR KA - A - NI
UḪ DINGIR-ID-MULU-ŠUB-TIG KI-A DINGIR-ID -MULU-ŠUB-TIG
ŠA - GAR LIG - GA - BI
UR-BI U-ME-NI-ŠAR-ŠAR BUR-TA U-ME-NI-LU
ŠU - EL - LA - ZU - TA U - ME - NI - LU - LU

COL. IV.

. . . . [SAG] - KI ID - KAB - BU
. . . . [SAG] - KI - BI U - ME - NI - KEŠDA
. . . SAG NI ŠA-A SIG (?) . . . DA U-ME-NI-NU-NU
. . . SAG-KI ID-ZI-DA *III* SAG-KI ID-KAB-BU
. . . . DINGIR-MU-BI SAG-KI-BI U-ME-NI-KEŠDA
. . . . . ḪE-EN-TIL-LA KI-BI-KU NA-AN-GE-GE
[ŠU- * ŠAG]-GA DINGIR-RA-NA-KU ḪE-EN-ŠI-IN-GE-GE

. . . . NAM - TA - E
. . . . *it - ta - ṣa - a*
. . . . „ „ NAM - TA - E
. . . . [NAM] - TA - E
. . . . [*it - ta*] - *ṣa - a*
. . . . [NAM] - TA - E
. . . . [*it - ta*] - *ṣa - a*
. . . . [NAM] - TA - E
. . . . *šu* (?) *iṭ - ḫu - u*
. . . . MU - UN - NA - TE
. . . . *iṭ - ḫu - u*
. . . . [IM] - MA - AN - SUM
. . . . [*ip*] - *pa - lis - ma*

200. "MULU-GIŠGAL-LU, ḪAR-ḪAR, KUR-KUR,
"The seeds of the plant *GURU UŠ RIG AN-BAR KA-A-NI,
"The foam of the Goddess Id, the earth of the Goddess Id,
"When he is very hungry (?),
"Mix up together, mash up in oil,
205. "With thy clean hand mash it up

COL. IV.

". . . . . the left temple (?)
". . . . . bind his temples (?)
". . . the hair of a . . . do thou plait and
"[Three on] his right temple (?), three on his left
". . . . . bind his temples (?)
"[That that man] may live, and unto his place it may not return,
"Into the kindly hands of his god may he be commended."

[Incantation :—]
[An evil . . . .] hath gone forth,
215. . . . . hath gone forth,
. . . . hath gone forth,
. . . . hath gone forth,
220. . . . . hath approached,
. . . . hath approached,
225. [Marduk] hath seen (him) and

. . . . ŠU - U - ME - TI
. . . . *li - ḳi - ma*
ERIN . . . . [ŠU] - U - ME - TI
e - rin . . . . *li - ḳi - ma*
ŠU - SAR *III* - A - [AN] . . . . [U-ME-NI-NU]-NU
pi - kur - ti šu - uš - lu - [uš . . . ṭi] - me - ma
KA-SAR *VII*-NA A-DU-*II*-[A-AN] U-ME-NI-KEŠDA
ki - ṣir si - bit a - di ši - na ku - ṣur - ma
NAM - ŠUB NUN - KI - GA U - ME - NI - SUM
ši - pat ^{alu}*Eridi i - di - ma*
SAG - MULU - TUR - RA - GE U - ME - NI - KEŠDA
ḳaḳ - ḳa - di mar - ṣi ru - [ku] - us - ma
UTUG - ḪUL A - LA - ḪUL BAR - KU ḪE - IM - TA - GUB
UTUG- * ŠIG-GA ALAD- * ŠIG-GA ḪE-EN-LAḪ-LAḪ-GI-EŠ

Duppu IX $^{KAM\text{-}ME}$ SAG-GIG-GA-MEŠ ZAG-TIL-LA-BI-KU

Ekal $^{m\ ilu}$*Aššur-bani-apli šar kiššati šar* $^{matu\ ilu}$*Aššuri* ^{KI}

(Etc.)

---

[a] *Piḳurtu*, according to Jensen (*ZK.*, i, 321; cf. ii, 25), means *bluthenrispe*, but this seems doubtful. He draws his conclusions principally from the Sixth Tablet of the Series *Shurpu* (*W.A.I.*, iv, 7):

"As this *pikurtu* is shredded and is cast into the fire,
"And the Fire-god devoureth it;
"Its *arê* will not return to its palm-tree,
"Nor will it be used in the process of dyeing."

As Jensen says, *pikurtu* is to be referred to the Aram. root *p'kar*,

"Take . . . . and
"Take cedar . . . . and
"Plait a triple cord[a] . . . and
"Tie twice seven knots and
"Perform the Incantation of Eridu and
"Bind the head of the sick man,
"That the evil Spirit, the evil Demon may stand aside,
"And a kindly Spirit, a kindly Genius be present."

TABLET IX OF THE SERIES "HEADACHE"
COMPLETE.

[Colophon.]

"to bind." In the Fifth Tablet of the Series *Maqlu* (l. 54), a *pikurtu ša ḳadišâti* is mentioned. In the present text the magician is directed to "take cedar . . . . . . , and weave a triple *pikurtu*, tying twice seven knots in it." Now, taking into consideration that the Aram. *p'kar* means "to bind," it seems most probable that *pikurtu* is a cord of fibre. The Shurpu text must then be translated, "As this cord is unravelled . . . . , its fibres will not return to its palm-tree," and in the Maqlu tablet it is certainly plausible that the *pikurti* of the sacred temple-women are the cords mentioned in Baruch vi, 43. The palm fibre is a material still used in the making of ropes in Assyria.

Tablet "P."

OBVERSE.

(PLATE XXV.)

[EN SAG] - GIG E - KUR - TA NAM - TA - [E]
[ṭi - '] - u ul - tu e - kur it - ta - ṣa - [a]

[E - DINGIR - EN] - LIL - LA - TA NAM - TA - [E]
[ul] - tu bît ilu Bêli it - ta - ṣa - a

[DINGIR-RAB]-KAN-ME : *la-bar-tum pa-rit-tum* :
KA-ṢIR[1]-NI-KU . . .

[U] - NU - KU - KU U - NU - ŠAR - ŠAR - DA
ul u - ša - aṣ - lal šit - ta[2] *ul uš - ṭa - a*[3] *- bi*

[TUR]-RA (?) GIG-U-NA : *mu-ru-uṣ mu-ši u ur-ra šu-u* :
E[4]-NE-BI-DA-GE

[SAG] - BI GIŠGAL - LU ALAM - BI URU - A - AN
ḳaḳ - ḳa[5] *- su a-lu-u la-an-šu a-bu-bu-um-ma*

[SUḪ]-BI ANA ŠU-ŠU[6]-RU : *zi-mu-šu šamu(u) up-pu-ti*[7]

[IGI - BI] GIŠ - TIR GIŠ - GIG NI - LAL - E
[pa] - nu - šu ṣil - li[8] *kiš - te*[9] *ḫa - aṣ - bu*[10]

[ŠU-BI GIŠ]-EŠ-SA-AD GIR-BI GIŠ-RAB-MAḪ . . .
[ḳat]-su na aḫ-ba-lu[11] *še-ip-šu lub-lu-bu*[3]*-um-ma*

. . . SA - NE ḪE - EN - ŠI - IN - IL - [LA]
. . . *bu - a - nu*[12] *mu - ḫa - am - me - ṭu na - [šu - u]*

Tablet "P."

Obverse.

(Plate XXV.)

Incantation :—

Headache from the Underworld hath gone forth,
Issuing from the Abode of Bel.
A rushing[a] hag-demon,
Granting no rest, nor giving kindly sleep.
It is the sickness of night and day,
Whose head is that of a demon,
Whose shape is as the Whirlwind ;
Its appearance is as the darkening heavens,
And its face as the deep shadow of the forest.
Its hand is a snare, its foot is a trap (?),
. . . a burning muscle raiseth.

---

[1] 46,301 apparently omits KA-ṢIR.
[2] 46,301, *tum*.
[3] 46,301 omits.
[4] 46,301, UD.
[5] 46,301 inserts *ad*.
[6] 46,301 inserts UŠ.
[7] 46,301, [*ša*]-*mu-u up-pu-tu*.
[8] 46,301, *lu*.
[9] 46,301, *ti*.
[10] 46,301, *bi*.
[11] 46,301, *lum*.
[12] 46,301, *ni*.

[a] *Parittum* (= *paridtum* or *parittum*). Cf. Syr. *p'rad*, fugit (Brockelmann, p. 285*a*).

[GIŠ-GI-EN-GI-NA] : *bi-na-a-ti*[1] *u-ḫa-am-maṭ*[2] : IN-BIL-BIL . . .

. . . . BUL - E SU MU - UN - DA - AB - ZI - [ZI]
. . . *ri u - na - aš*[3] *zu - mur u - šaḫ - ḫa - aḫ*

. . . . GIM ? MU - UN - DA - AB - GE - GE
. . *ṭi-'-i ša ki-ma kar-pa-ti ša-ḫar-ra-ti*[4] *u-ša-aš-ga-mu*

. . . [*u*]*-kan-na-an bu-a-nu i-ṣa-ar* : SA ŠI-IN . .[5]

. . . [*a-me*]*-lu ki-ma i-bi-ḫi*[6] *i-ṣa-ar* : AL-SUR-RA

. . .[7] *ut* (?) *- ni u - kan - na - an* : AN - ḪUM - MU

. . . *pa* (?)*-a ap-pa kima it-ti-e i-sik*[8]*-kir* : AN[9]-UŠ-SA

. . . KU ? GIM : *up-pa*[10] *a-ḫi kima pu-uḳ-li*[11] *i-tar-rak* : ŠI-IN-ḲU-ḲU-E

. . . [IM]-GIŠGAL-LU[12] (?)-GU-GIM ŠI-IN-TAR . . .
[*rit*][13] *- ta ki - ma ḳi - e me - ḫi - e i - par - ra - '*

MURGU-GIM KI-A : *pu-u-da kima kib-ri 'u-ab-bat* : ŠI-IN . . . E

GABA GI-ḪA-AN-GIM : *ir-tum kima* ^kanu^ *ḫi-in-nu i-šal-laṭ* : AN-SIL-SIL . . . E

ṪIL-TIL GIŠ-MA-SUN-GIM IN-DAK-DAK[14] . . . .
ṣi-la-ni kima e-lip-pi la-bir-ti i-na-ḳar

ŠA-MAḪ ŠA-SIG-GA[15] ŠU-MU-UN-DIB-DIB . . . .
ša - [maḫ] - ḫu kima ir - ri ḳaṭ - ni i - ṣab - tu

Scorching the members,
Shaking the limbs (?), wasting the body,
A sickness which shatters (?) [the members] like an earthen pot,
Minishing [the muscles], weakening the sinews,
Weakening the whole man (?) like . . . (?)
Minishing the . . . . .
Choking the nostrils as with pitch,
Bursting through the ribs (?) like tow,[a]
Breaking the fingers as a rope of wind.
It destroyeth the flanks like a river-bank (?),
It splitteth the breast in twain like a stalk of henna,
It crusheth the sides like an old ship,
It seizeth on the stout-hearted like little . . .[b]

---

[1] 46,301, *tu*.
[2] 46,301 . . . *ṭu*.
[3] 46,301, *a-šu*.
[4] 46,301, *kar-pat ša-ḫar-rat*.
[5] 46,301, RU (?)-E.
[6] 46,301, *e-bi-ḫu*.
[7] 46,301, *ma* . . . .
[8] 46,301, *sak*.
[9] 46,301 inserts *nu*.
[10] 46,301, *pu*.
[11] 46,301, *lu*.
[12] 46,301 omits.
[13] From 46,301, which has *rit-tu*.
[14] 46,301 ends the line with this character.
[15] 46,301, GIM.

[a] *Puḳlu* is the Chaldee *pûḳlâ* (Levy, *Chald. Wörterb.*, ii, p. 284). *Uppa aḫi*, "the *uppa* of the side," is of uncertain meaning.

[b] *Irri* is some part of the body (see Jensen, *Mythen*, p. 456). *Šamaḫḫu* is doubtful.

ḲU-DA U-GUG-GIM : *ši-i-ḫu kima*[1] *ur-ba-ti uš-na-al* : BA-[AN-NA]-A

MU GUD-GIM : *ra-ba-a kima*[2] *al-pi i-pal-lik* : TIG-NI-RA-RA

GUD NI-RA : *al-pa*[3] *im-ḫaṣ-ma al-pi ul ip-di* : GUD-NA NU-IL-LA

AM NI-RA : *ri-i-mi im-ḫaṣ-ma ri-mi ul u-pa-šiḫ* : AM-NA[4] NU-ŠED-DE

DARA NI-RA SI-BI NU-MU-UN-SU-UB-SU-UB
[*tu*]-*ra-ḫu im-ḫaṣ*[5]*-ma ḳar-ni*[6]*-šu ul u-šak-lil*

(PLATE XXVI.)

SIḲḲA SIḲḲA-BAR-RA NI-RA ZUR-BI NU-MU-UN-ZUR-ZUR-RI
a-tu-du šap-[*pa-ru*] *im-ḫaṣ-ma bu-ur-šu-nu ul u-kan-ni*[7]

GAR-UR-* TATTAB-MA EDIN-NA NI-RA GIŠ-SAR-AMAŠ-* DIRIG-GA-[GIM] UR-BI MU-UN-DU-DU
bu-ul ṣi-ri im-ḫaṣ-ma ki-ma ki-ri-e ša ḫa-ru-u na-as-ḫu išteniš(*niš*) *it-ta-kip*

GIŠ-ŠUB-GIR-GIM GAR-NAM MU-UN-ŠI-IN-LAL-E
ki-ma mit-pa-a[4]*-nu ba-aš-me*[8] *mimma šum-šu i-sak-kir*

DINGIR-SILIG-MULU-ŠAR : *ilu Marduk ip-pa*[9]*-lis-su-ma* : IGI-IM-MA-AN-SUM

It bendeth low the lofty like a reed,
It cutteth off the mighty like an ox.
Smiting oxen, it spareth not the herds,
Smiting wild bulls, it giveth them no rest,
Smiting the mountain-goat so that it completeth not its horn,[a]

(Plate XXVI.)

Smiting ibex and goat so that they guard not their offspring,
Smiting the beasts of the desert so that they run wild,
Like a garden whereof the ditch hath been removed,
As with the fangs (?) of a viper it shutteth up everything.[b]
Marduk hath seen him, and

---

1 46,301, *ki*-[*ma*].
2 46,301, *ki-ma*.
3 46,301, *pi*.
4 46,301 omits.
5 46,301, [*ḫa*]-*aṣ*.
6 46,301, *na-a*.
7 46,301, *na*.
8 46,301, *mu*.
9 46,301, *pal*.

a I.e., because the growth of the ibex, up to about five years, can be reckoned by the nodules which project along the front of the horns.

b The meaning of this line is obscure, firstly because we do not know what is meant by the expression "the bow of the viper," and secondly *isakkir* is doubtful. The sense may be that nothing can be produced by reason of the disease, and if so *isakkir* is to be compared in sense to the Hebrew סָגַר in 1 Sam. i, 5, "the Lord had shut up her womb."

A-A-NI DINGIR-EN-KI-RA E-A BA-ŠI-IN-TU GU-MU-UN-NA-AN-DA-A[1]

a-na a-bi-šu ^ilu^*E-a a-na bîti i-ru-um-ma i-šis-si*

A-A-MU SAG-GIG E-KUR-TA NAM-TA-E

a-bi ṭi-' ul-tu e-kur it-ta-ṣa-a

A-DU *II*-KAN : *a-di ši-na iḳ*[2]*-bi-šum-ma* : AŠ-U-UB-DA[3]

A-NA[4] IB[5]-ŠA-A NA-BI NU-UN[6]-ZU[7] A-NA NI-IB-GE-GE[8]

mi-na-a e[9]*-pu-uš amelu*[10] *šu-a-tu*[11] *ul i-di ina mi-ni-i*[12] *i-pa-aš-šaḫ*

REVERSE.

DINGIR-EN-KI DU-NI DINGIR-SILIG-MULU-ŠAR MU-UN-NA-NI-IB-GE-GE

^ilu^*E-a mâri*[13]*-šu* ^ilu^*Marduk ip-pal*

DU-MU A-NA NU-NI-ZU A-NA RA-AB-DAḪ-A[14]

ma-a[6]*-ri mi-na-a la ti*[9]*-di mi-na-a lu-rad-di*[15]*-ka*

DINGIR-SILIG-MULU-ŠAR A-NA NU-NI-ZU A-NA RA-AB-DAḪ-A[16]

^ilu^*Marduk mi-na-a la ti-di mi-na-a lu-rad-di-ka*

GAR-GA-E NI-ZU-A-MU : *ša ana-ku i-du-u at-ta ti-i-di* : [17]ZA-E IN-GA-E-ZU

GIN-NA DU-MU : *a-lik ma-ri* ^ilu^*Marduk* : DINGIR-SILIG-MULU-ŠAR

Into the house of Ea his father hath entered and spoken,
"Father, the Headache from the Underworld hath gone forth."
Twice he hath said unto him,
"What this man shall do he knoweth not whereby he may be relieved."

REVERSE.

Ea hath answered his son Marduk,
"O my son, what dost thou not know, what more can I give thee?
"O Marduk, what dost thou not know, what can I add unto thy knowledge?
"What I know, thou knowest also.
"Go, my son Marduk,

[1] 46,301 and K. 4,840, DE-E.
[2] 46,301, *ḳi.*
[3] 46,301, KA.
[4] 46,301 inserts NI.
[5] 46,301 inserts BA.
[6] 46,301 omits.
[7] 46,301 inserts NA.
[8] 46,301 apparently BA-GE-GE; K. 4,840, BA-NI-IB-GE-GE.
[9] 46,301, *i.*
[10] 46,301, *a-me-lu.*
[11] 46,301, MU-*a-tim.*
[12] 46,301, *mi-na-a* for *ina mi-ni-i.*
[13] 46,301, *ma-ra.*
[14] 46,301 and K. 4,840, E.
[15] 46,301 and K. 4,840, *uṣ-ṣip.*
[16] 46,301, E.
[17] 46,301 inserts U.

[GIŠ ?]-BA-AN-GAB-GAB[1]-LAL-E GIŠ-GAM-MA : „[2]-*e*
^{isu}*kip-pa-ti li-ḳi-ma* : ŠU-U-ME-TI

ID-KA-A-NA-TA A-ŠU-BA[3] E-RI[4]-TI
ina pi-i na-ra-a-ti[5] *ki-lal-li-e mê*^{pl}[6] *li-ḳi-e-ma*

A-BI TU-AZAG-ZA-NA : *ana mê*^{pl}[6]*-šu-nu-ti*[7] *ši-pat-ka*
elliti(ti)[8] *i-di-ma* : U-ME-NI-SUM

TU-AZAG-ZA-NA : *ina te-e-ka el-li*[9] *ul-lil-ma* :
U-ME-NI-RI

[A-BI MULU]-GIŠGAL-LU DU-DINGIR-RA-NA U-ME-NI-SU
me-e šu-nu-ti[7] *a-me-lu mâr ili-šu zu*[10]*-lu-uḫ*[11]*-ma*

. . . . ZU-NA SAG-GA-NA U-ME-NI-KEŠDA
ina ši-ti-ik . . li ḳaḳ-ḳa[12]*-su ru-ku-us-ma*

U-I-KAM : *ûmu(mu) ak-kal liš-tab-ri*[13] :
KAN-NI-IB-ZAL-ZAL-E[14]

AN-MUNSUB-AN-NA-TA : *ina ši-me*[15]*-tan pu-ru-'-ma* :
U-ME-NI-TAR

SILA-DAGAL-LA-KU : *ina ri-bi-ti i-di-ma* : U-ME-NI-ŠUB

SAG-GIG SAG-GA-NA ḪE-IM-MA-AN-ŠED-[DE]
ṭi-'-u[16] *ša ḳaḳḳadi*[17]*-šu lip-ta-[šaḫ]*[18]

---

[1] 46,301 inserts ID.

[2] 46,301 reads for this line . . *e a-lal-li-e iṣ-ṣi kip-pa-tum li-ḳi-e-[ma]*.

[3] 46,301, BI.

[4] 46,301, RI-E for E-RI.

"Take a bundle of twigs (?),[a] and
"At the confluence of two streams take thou water and
"Perform thy pure incantation over this water, and
"With thy pure exorcism cleanse and
"With this water sprinkle the man, son of his god and
"Bind it upon his head with . . . .
"When he eats[b] let him be sated:
"At eventide cut it off and
"Cast it into the broad places
"That the sickness of his head may be assuaged, and

[5] 46,301, *nârâli*^{pl}.
[6] 46,301, *me-e*.
[7] 46,301, *tu*.
[8] 46,301, *tim*.
[9] 46,301, *lu*.
[10] 46,301, *su*.
[11] 46,301, *luḫ*.
[12] 46,301 inserts *ad*.
[13] 46,301, *ru*.
[14] 46,301 omits.
[15] 46,301, *mi*.
[16] 46,301, *i*.
[17] 46,301, *ḳak-ḳa-di*.
[18] 46,301, *liš-tap-šiḫ*.

[a] The variant gives *alallî iṣṣi kippatum*. *Kippatu* occurs in the phrase *kippat ḫuḫari* (*W.A.I.*, v, 26, 59), "the *kippatu* of a bird-trap," and therefore *kippatu* cannot be the name for a certain kind of wood or tree. It is probably the same word as the Hebrew *kippâ*, a branch or twig, and if so, the *kippat ḫuḫari* will be the small piece of wood which props up the door or lid of the trap. In the case of *alallî kippati* or *alallî iṣṣi kippatum*, "an *alallu* of twigs," *alallu* is to be referred to the root *alâlu*, "to bind," i.e., a bundle. See also Tablet "A A," l. 63.

[b] The same phrase occurs in Tablet "D," l. 29. The translation is, however, doubtful.

SAG-GIG A-AN-GIG-GAB-BA-GIM ḪA-BA-RA-AN-ZI . .
mu-ru-uṣ ḳaḳ-ḳa-di[1] *ša ki-ma zu-un-ni*[2] *mu-ši kit-mu-ru li-in-*[*na-siḫ*]

I DINGIR-EN-KI-GE PA-E-ḪE-[A-GE[3]]
a-mat ^{ilu}*E-a*[4] *liš-te-pi*

DINGIR-DAM-GAL-NUN-NA SI-ḪE-EN[5]-SI-DI-E
^{ilu}*Dam-ki*[6]*-na liš-te-šir*

DINGIR-SILIG-?-NUN-NA DU-SAG-ZU-AB-GE *ŠAG[7]-GA TAG-BI-ZA-A-[KAN]
^{ilu}*Marduk mar riš-tu-u ša ap-si-i bu-un-nu u du-um*[8]*-mu-ḳu*[9] *ku-um-mu*

. . . . SAG-GIG-GA A . . . .

. . . ANA-GIM I EDIN-NA NUN-KI DA-NU-UB . . .

"That the Headache which like the dew hath fallen, may be removed.
"May the Word of Ea make clear,
"May Damkina direct aright.
"O Marduk, eldest son of the Deep!
"Thine is the power to brighten and bless!"

[PRAYER] OF THE SICK HEAD . . . .

---

[1] 46,301, *du*.
[2] 46,301, *nu*.
[3] 46,301, PA-Ḫ̮E-E-A . .
[4] 46,301, *Ea*.
[5] 46,301, AN.
[6] 46,301 inserts *an*.
[7] 46,301, *ŠIG.
[8] 46,301, *dum* for *du-um*.
[9] 46,301, *ḳa*.

Inim-inim-ma alam-gar-sag-il-la im-ma-gé.

Tablet "R."

OBVERSE.

(PLATE XXIX.)

EN NAM-TAR ḪUL-IK KALAM-MA BIL-GIM MU-[MU]
ša ma-a-tu ki-ma i-ša-tu i-ḳam-mu-u
NAM-TAR AZAG-GIM MULU-RA TE-A
ša ki-ma a-šak-ku ana ameli i-ṭi-iḫ-ḫu-[u]
NAM-TAR DINGIR EDIN-NA LIL-GIM NI-SIR-SIR
ša ina ṣi-rim ki-ma za-ḳi-ḳi it-ta-na-aš-rab-bi-ṭu
NAM-TAR ḪUL-LU-GIM MULU-RA BA-AN-UR-UR
ša ki-ma lim-ni ameli iḫ-ḫa-zu
NAM-TAR DUB-ME-GIM MULU-RA BA-DUB
ša ki-ma li-i-bu ameli i-li-'-i-bu
NAM-TAR ŠU NU-TUK GIR NU-TUK MULU-A GIG-A GIN-GIN
ša ga-ta la i-šu-u še-ip la i-šu-u mut-tal-lik mu-ši
NAM-TAR MULU-TUR-RA GA-RAS-SIR-GIM BA-AN-GAM
mar-ṣa ki-ma ka-ra-ši iḫ-ta-ra-as
GIŠ-GI-EN-GI-NA BA-NI-IN-SIR
bi-na-[a-ti-šu] uk-tas-si
GUD-DA U . . . . BA-NI-IN-NA
mi-la-šu . . . . uš-ni-il

Prayer of the Figure of his Bodily Form in Clay.

Tablet "R."

OBVERSE.

(PLATE XXIX.)

Incantation :—

O Plague-god that devoureth the land like fire,
Plague-god that attacketh a man like a fever,
Plague-god that roameth like the wind over the desert,
Plague-god that seizeth on a man like an evil thing,
Plague-god that tormenteth the man like a plague,
Plague-god that hath no hands nor feet, that wandereth by night,
Plague-god that teareth the sick man in shreds like a leek,
That hath bound his members,
That hath brought low his full strength [like a plant (?)],

[GIŠ]-NA GIG-U-[NA-GE NU-MU]-UN-DA-KU-KU

[*ina*] *ma-a-a-*[*li-šu ina šat mu-ši ul*] *i-ṣal-lal*

. . . ALAM (?) *ŠIG-GA . . . . . . NE-IN-LAL

. . . . *la* (?) *- an - šu . . . . u - kan - niš*

PAP - ḪAL - LA - KU NE - IN - DIB

pu - ri - di - šu iṣ - ṣa - bat

DINGIR - BI ID - BI BA - NI - IN - BAD

ilu - šu it - ti - šu it - te - si

AMA-DINGIR-NINNI-A-NI SU-NI-TA BA-NI-IN-SU-SU

ilu Iš - tar - šu ina zu - um - ri - šu ir - te - iḳ

DINGIR - SILIG - MULU - ŠAR IGI : GAR - GA - E : GIN - NA DU - MU

IM - ZU - AB - TA U - ME - NI - KID

ḳi - ri - iṣ - ma

REVERSE.

(PLATE XXX.)

ALAM GAR - SAG - IL - LA - A - NI U - ME - NI - DIM

ṣa - lam an du - na - ni - šu bi - ni - ma

UR MULU-TUR-RA-GE GIG-U-NA U-ME-NI-NA

IT-TIG-ZI-GA-TA SU-NI-TA U-ME-TE-GUR-GUR

ina še - ri zu - mur - šu kup - pir - ma

NAM - ŠUB NUN - KI - GA U - ME - NI - SUM

ŠI DINGIR-BABBAR-KU IGI-NI U-ME-NI-GAR

ana ma-ḫar e-rib ilu Šamši(ši) pa-ni-šu šu-kun-ma

NAM - TAR ḪUL - IK DIB - BA - A - NI - TA BAR - KU ḪE - IM - TA - GUB

ka - mu - šu ina a - ḫa - a - ti li - iz - ziz

[At night] on his bed he cannot sleep,
It hath subjected . . . .
It hath seized on his loins,[a]
His god is far distant from him,
His goddess from his body is afar.
Marduk hath seen him (etc.),
"What I" (etc.),
"Go, my son (Marduk),
"Pull off a piece of clay from the deep,

REVERSE.

(PLATE XXX.)

"Fashion a figure of his bodily form (therefrom) and
"Place it on the loins of the sick man by night,
"At dawn make the 'atonement' for his body,
"Perform the Incantation of Eridu,
"Turn his face to the west,
"That the evil Plague-demon which hath seized upon him
"May vanish away from him."

[a] *Puridu*, see Jensen, *Mythen und Epen*, p. 508.

[INIM]-INIM-MA ALAM-GAR-SAG-IL-LA IM-MA-GE[1]

[EN] . . . . . ḪUŠ . . . .
. . . . NA . . . .

[Colophon.]

[1] Tablet "S" (K. 3,518).

REVERSE.

. . . .
. . ZU - AB - TA . . . .
ALAM - A - NI . . . .
ṣa - lam - šu ṣal - ma . . . .
SIG - UZ - BABBAR SIG - UZ - GIG SAG - GA . . . . . .
ina ḳaḳ - ḳa - di - [šu] . . .
SU MULU - TUR - RA GE U - ME . . . .
NAM - ŠUB DINGIR - EN - KI - GE U - ME - [NI - SUM]
ŠI DINGIR - BABBAR - ŠU-A IGI - NI U - ME - NI - [GAR]
UTUG - U - DIB - BA - A - NI BAR - KU ḪE - [IM - TA - GUB]
ša ut - tu - šu [ina a - ḫa - a - ti li - iz - ziz]
NAM - TAR ḪUL - DIB - BA - NI BAR - KU NI . . . .
ka - mu - šu ana a - ḫa - a - tu li - [iz - ziz]

INIM - INIM - MA ALAM - GAR - SAG - IL - LA . . .

EN UTUG-ḪUL-EDIN-NA BAR-NE NA BAR MULU . . .
ana mul - te - piš - u - ti za - mar . . .

[Colophon.]

PRAYER OF THE FIGURE OF HIS BODILY FORM IN CLAY.[a]

. . . .

[Colophon.]

---

[a] Tablet "S" begins in the same way as Tablet "R," but the ending is different :—

REVERSE.

" [Pull off a piece] of [clay ?] from the deep,
" [Fashion] a black figure [of his bodily form],
" [Bind] on his head the hair of a white goat,
" And the hair of a black goat,
" Place it on the body of the sick man,
" Perform the Incantation of Ea,
" [Turn] his face to the west,
" That the Spirit which hath glanced at him [may stand] aside,
" And the evil Plague-demon which hath seized upon him
" May vanish away from him."

PRAYER OF THE IMAGE OF HIS BODILY FORM [IN CLAY ?].

Incantation :—" The evil Spirit hath laid in wait in the desert
" Unto the side of the man [hath drawn nigh]."

Inim-inim-ma alam-gar-sag-il-la ku-še-kan.

Tablet "T."

OBVERSE.

(PLATE XXXI.)

[EN] UTUG-ḪUL EDIN-NA BAR-NE NA BAR MULU . . .
u-tuk-ku lim-nu ina ṣi-ri ir-bi-iṣ . . .

ALAD-ḪUL SAG-UŠ SAG-BA-AN-KIL-BA MULU . . .
[*še*] - *id - du lim - nu ka - a - a - na ip - rik - ma ma - am - ma* . . . .

[GIDIM]-ḪUL EDIN-NA MU-UN-SA-SA MULU ŠA-KU-[GU-GA] . . .
e-kim-mu lim-nu ina ṣi-rim i-ku-uš-ma ša-ga-ša . .

MULLA-ḪUL ERI-A MU-UN-GUB-GUB KALAM-MA GAZ ŠA-A . . . .
gal-lu-u lim-nu ina ali i-da-al ana ša-ga-aš ni-ši ul i-ga- . . .

GURUŠ-RA MU-UN-GE-GE-NE : *id-lu i-šab-bi-ṭu*

[KI-EL-RA] MU-UN-DUB-DUB-BU-NE : *ar-da-tum i-nap-pa-ṣu*

[TUR-TUR-RA G]A[1] -RAS-SIR-GIM MU-UN- ? - ? -E-NE
[*ṣi-iḫ-ḫi-ru*][1] *-ti ki-ma ka-ra-šu* . . . . *-šu-u*

. . . . LIKIR MU - UN - [SIR - SIR] - E - NE
. . . . *lib - ba i* - [*na - as*] - *sa - ḫu*

Prayer of the Figure of his Bodily Form in Dough.

Tablet "T."

OBVERSE.

(PLATE XXXI.)

Incantation :—

The evil Spirit hath lain in wait in the desert
unto the side of the man [hath drawn nigh],
The evil Genius for ever is rampant
And none can [resist him],
The evil Ghost goeth furtively in the desert and
[Causeth] slaughter [among men].
The evil Devil prowleth in the city,
[It hath no rest ?] from slaughtering men.
They smite the hero,
They lay low the maiden,
The little ones like a leek they tear in pieces,
They tear out the heart . . . .

---

[1] Inserted from the copy in *W.A.I.*, iv, 16.

. . . . [A-LA]-GIM IM-[MA-AN]-DUL-E-NE
. . . . *[kima] a - li - e i - kat - ta - mu*
. . . . GABA - IM - MA - AN - RI - EŠ
. . . . LA (?)-GIM PA-KAD-DU MU-NI-IN-AG-GI-EŠ
. . . . *it-ta-na-aš-šib [kima] ka-mi-i i-ta-ru-šu*
. . . . NA E-A-NI-KU IM-MA-AN-UŠ EŠ : *ir-du-šu*
. . . . . [IM]-MA-AN-DA-KUR SU-GIR-RA BA-NA
. . . . . *it - te - kir ina ru - šum - ti na - di*
. . . . ZI - ZI ID NU - UN - GE - GE
. . . . . *ul ina - aš - ši a - ḫi - šu ul u - [tar]*
U [NU-UN-DA]-AN-KU-E A NU-UN-DA-AN-NAK-[E]
a-ka-[li] a-ka-la ul i-li-'-i me-e ša-ta-a ul i-li-['-i]
GIS-GI-EN-GI-NA-BI BA-BIR-BIR-RI-EŠ SU-BI ŠAR-ŠI DA-BA-AN-[SUM]
bi-na-ti-šu us-sap-pi-ḫu zumur-šu da-um-ma-tu um-tal-li
DINGIR-SILIG-MULU-ŠAR IGI : GAR-GA-E : GIN-NA DU-MU
DUG-SAR-RA A U-ME-NI-SUM : *me-e mul-li-ma*
ŠINIG U-IN-NU-UŠ GIŠIMMAR-DU GI-SUL-ŠAR RIG-LI
ERIN - BABBAR - RA ŠA - BI U - ME - NI - SUM
NAM - ŠUB NUN - KI - GA U - MU - E - NI - ŠID
A - BI NAM - ŠUB ŠU - GAL U - MU - E - NI - DU
me - e šip - ti ra - biš šuk - lil - ma
MU - AZAG - ZA - NA U - MU - E - NI - DU
A-BI MULU-GIŠGAL-LU U-MU-E-NI-SUM : *a-me-lu šu-luḫ-ma*

Like a demon they envelop . . . .
They draw near . . . . . .
[Where ?] he sitteth they turn him back like a shut gate (?),[a]
Unto his house they drive him . . . .
. . . is estranged (?), he falleth in the marsh.
He cannot lift [his limbs], nor turn his side.
He hath no desire to eat food,
Nor drink water,
His members are dissolved, and his body is filled with pain.
Marduk hath seen him (etc.),
" What I " (etc.),
" Go, my son (Marduk),
" Fill a pot with water and
" *Bînu* the *maštakal*-plant, *suḫuššu*, a stalk of *šalalu*,[b] cypress,
" And white cedar put therein and
" Perform the Incantation of Eridu and
" Make perfect the water of the Incantation and
" Make perfect thy pure exorcism,
" Sprinkle the man with the water and

---

[a] The translation of this line is doubtful.

[b] *Šalalu* is possibly to be compared to the Syriac ܦܠ (Payne Smith, *Thesaurus*, 4,163), an Indian drug something like ginger: *radix nymphææ loti.*

GAR-GAR-LAG-GA SAG-GA-NA U-ME-NI-GAR : *šu-kun-ma*

MULU-GIŠGAL-LU PAP-ḪAL-LA DU DINGIR-RA-NA U-ME-TE-GUR-GUR

kup-pir-ma

REVERSE.

(PLATE XXXII.)

ALAM-BI ZAG GIS . . . . KU-ŠE U-ME-[NI-ḪAR]

ṣa-lam-šu i-da-at-sa [ša] tap-pi-in-ni e-[ṣir-ma]

MULU-BI MUḪ-NA A U-ME-NI . . . .

ana eli ameli šu-a-tu me-e šu-bi-'-ma

A NAM-ŠIB-BA U-ME-NI-ŠU-NAG

GAR-NA GIBILLA U-ME-NI-E

A-SU-NA AN-TA-SUR-RA-TA

NAM-TAR SU-NI-TA A-GIM ḪE-IM-MA-AN-SUR-SUR-RA

A-BI DUK-KU U-MU-E-NI-ŠI-IN-GE

me-e-šu-nu-ti a-nạ kar-pa-ti tir-ma

SILA-DAGAL-LA-KU U-MU-UN-DUB : *ana ri-bi-ti tu-bu-uk-ma*

GAR-GIG-GA ID-BA-BA-GE SILA-DAGAL-LA ḪA-BA-AN-TUM

ma-ru-uš-tu ša e-mu-ḳi i-na-aš-ša-ru ri-bi-tu lit-bal

*UḪ GU-GU-GA-KAN A-GIM ḪE-IM-TA-BAL-E

ru-'-tum na-di-tum ši-i ki-ma me-e lit-ta-bi-ik

*UḪ-GU-GA *UḪ-A-DE-A BA-DA-AN-ŠAR A-GA-KU ḪE-EN-ŠI-IN-GE-GE

kiš-pu ša ina ru-'-ti na-di-ti bul-lu-lu ana ar-ka-ti li-tu-ru

" Set *li'i*-food at his head and
" Make the 'atonement' for the wanderer, the son of his god, and

REVERSE.

(PLATE XXXII.)

" Fashion a figure of him in dough,[a]
" Put water upon the man and
" Pour forth the water of the Incantation ;
" Bring forth a censer (and) a torch,
" As the water trickleth away from his body
" So may the pestilence in his body trickle away.
" Return these waters into a cup and
" Pour them forth in the broad places,
" That the evil influence which hath brought low (his) strength
" May be carried away into the broad places,
" That the spittle which hath been spat
" May be poured forth like the water,
" That the magic which mingleth with the spat-forth spittle
" May be turned back,

---

[a] *Tappinnu,* written ideographically KU - ŠE, and therefore evidently connected with corn. It occurs in another incantation (K. 5,266 and Bu. 89-4-26, 16) in the line *sibit akal tappinni elli liḳi*-[*ma*], "Take seven loaves of pure *tappinnu.*" Now since it can be moulded into figures, as in the text above, it is a plastic material, and, as we have shown, it is connected with corn, and loaves are made of it ; consequently *dough* is the obvious meaning. Although a common material among savage tribes for making magical figures, it has not been otherwise met with in the Assyrian texts. On the use of seven loaves of bread in Semitic magic, see Introduction.

MU - GU - GA I - DINGIR - EN - KI - GA - GE

SU- * UḪ-GIR-GE GU-DE KA-SAR-BI ḪE-EN-GABA-A

šap-tan mu-uṣ-ṣab-ra-tum ša i-ta-ma-a ri-kis-si-na lip-pa-ṭir

MULU-GIŠGAL-LU-BI ḪE-EN-EL ḪE-EN-LAḪ-LAḪ

SU- * ŠAG-GA DINGIR-RA-NA-KU ḪE-EN-ŠI-IN-GE-GE

INIM-INIM-MA ALAM GAR-SAG-IL-LA KU-ŠE-KAN

EN UTUG-ḪUL A-LA-ḪUL GIDIM-ḪUL MULLA-ḪUL SAG ITI NU-TIL-LA-ḪUL

kima labiri - šu ša - ṭir - ma ba - a - ri

"By the magic of the Word of Ea,
"The chanting lips which have uttered the ban,—
"May their bond be loosened!
"That this man may be pure, be clean!
"Into the kindly hands of his god may he be commended."

Prayer of the Figure of his Bodily Form in Dough.[a]

Incantation :—"Evil Spirit, evil Demon, evil Ghost, evil Devil, that bring evil at the beginning of an incomplete month."[b]

---

[a] Tablet "W" on pl. 36 is the remains of a similar text, but hardly anything is left.

[b] On the meaning of this, compare my *Reports*, vol. ii, p. xix.

Miscellaneous Incantations.

Tablet of the Evil Eye.

Tablet "U."

OBVERSE.

(PLATE XXXIII.)

. . . LAL-LAL . . . *-tum ka-sa-a-tu*[1] *a-a-lu-u ša ameli i-kat-tam* : GIŠGAL-LU MULU BA(?)-DUL

. . . . *dal-ḫa-a-tum ka-sa-[a]-tu* : GAR-LAL-A-AN

. . . . . *ka-ba-a-ti ša ma-a-tu* : KALAM-MA-GE

. . . . GIG-GA [:] *mu-šam-ri-ṣa a-tu*[1] *ša ni-ši* : NAM-MULU-GIŠGAL-LU-GE

[IGI-GAR-ḪU]L-GIM-MA [:] *i-ni li-mut-tum mut-tal-lik-tum* : PAP-ḪAL-LA-GE

[UB-KU AB]-ŠI-IN-BAR [:] *a-na tub-ḳa ip-pal*[2]*-lis-ma tub-ḳi u-ri-iḳ* : UB IM-SU

[DA-KU AB]-ŠI-IN-BAR [:] *ana ša-ḫat ip-pal*[2]*-lis-ma* [3]*ša-ḫat u-ri-iḳ* : DA IM-SU

[DAGAL KALAM-MA] AB-ŠI-IN-BAR : *ana*[4] *maš-tak ma-a-tu*[1] *ip-pal-lis*[2]*-ma maš-tak ma-a-tu u-ri-iḳ* : DAGAL KALAM-MA IM-SU

[MULU-GIŠGAL-LU]-PAP-ḪAL-LA-KU AB-ŠI-IN-BAR GIŠ-KUD-KUD-DA-GIM TIG-KI-A IM-MI-IN-GAM

ana a-me-lu mut-tal-li-ku ip-pal[2]*-lis-ma ki-ma iṣ-ṣi nak-su še-ib-ri ki-šad-su ur-da-du-ud*

DINGIR-EN-KI MULU-BI : *ilu Ea ameli* MU[5]*-a-tim i-mur-ma* : ŠI-U-NE-IN-GAB

Miscellaneous Incantations.

Tablet of the Evil Eye.

Tablet "U."

OBVERSE.

(PLATE XXXIII.)

The . . . which bindeth,
A demon which envelopeth the man,
The . . . bringing trouble, which bindeth,
The . . . heavy (?) upon the land,
Bringing sickness upon men,
The roving Evil Eye
Hath looked on the neighbourhood and hath vanished far away,
Hath looked on the vicinity and hath vanished far away,
Hath looked on the chamber of the land and hath vanished far away,
It hath looked on the wanderer
And like wood cut off for poles[a] it hath bent his neck.
Ea hath seen this man and

---

[a] *Šebru*, probably the same word as *šebiru*, part of a machine (the pole of a *shaduf* ?). According to *Cuneiform Texts*, part xii, pl. 44, l. 35, IṢ-ḪAS = *iṣu šebirum*, the Sumerian meaning "cut wood."

[1] 93,081, *ti*.
[2] 93,081, *pa*.
[3] 93,081 inserts *ana*.
[4] 93,081, *a-na*.
[5] 93,081, *šu-ma*.

GAR SAG-GA-NA : *a-ka-lu ina ḳaḳ-ḳa-di-šu iš-kun* :
MU-NI-IN-GAR

GAR SU-NA : *a-ka-lu ana zumri-šu u-ṭaḫ-ḫi* :
MU-NI-IN-TE

? NE NAM - TIL - LA - GE MU - UN - NA - AN ?
ik - ri - bi ba - la - ṭu i - kar - rab - šu

[MULU]-GIŠGAL-LU DU DINGIR-RA-NA : *amelu mâr*
ili-šu at-ta : ZA-E-ME-EN

[GAR SAG]-DU : *a-ka-lu ša ina ḳaḳ-ḳa-di-ka*
u-ṭaḫ-ḫu-u : [MU-NI]-IN-TE-A-TA

[GAR SU]-ZU : *a-ka-lu ša zu-mur-ka u-kap-pi-ru* :
. . . ŠUB-BA . . . .

[. .]-ZU ḪE-EN-IB-SIG-GA ZA-E-ME-EN NAM-ṬIL-[LA]
[mu]-ru (?)-*uṣ-ka lip-šaḫ-ma at-ta bu-lu-[uṭ]*

[KI - NAM] - TIL - LA - GE GIR - ZU GUB - BU - NE
[ina ḳaḳ]-ḳa-ru ba-la-ṭu še-ip-ka li-iz-ziz

[MULU]-GIŠGAL-LU DU DINGIR-RA-NA ZA-E-ME-EN
[a] - me - lu ma - ri ili - šu at - ta

[IGI] GAR-GIG-GA : *i-ni ša ana ma-ru-uš-tum*
ip-pal-su-ka : MU-UN-ŠI-IN-BAR-RA . . .

[IGI] GAR-ḪUL-GIM-MA : *i-ni ša ana limuttim(tim)*
ip-pal-su-ka : MU-UN-ŠI-IN-BAR-RA . . .

. . . RA - GE : *ša ina a* - . . . .

REVERSE.

. . . . GE . . . .

. . . . *- a - lu* . . . .

. . . . BAD - GA . . . .

. . . . *la ḳa - ni - e* . . . .

[DINGIR]-DA-MU URUDU-ŠUN-TAB-BA ḪU-MU-UN-SIG-GA
ilu Ba'u ina pa - aš - tum li - im - ḫa - aṣ . .

Hath placed food at his head,

Hath brought food nigh to his body,

Hath shown favour for his life—

Thou man, son of his god,

May the food which I have brought to thy head—

May the food with which I have made an "atonement" for thy body

Assuage thy sickness, and thou be restored,

That thy foot may stand in the land of life;[a]

Thou man, son of his god,

The Eye which hath looked on thee for harm,

The Eye which hath looked on thee for evil,

Which in . . . .

REVERSE.

. . . .

May Ba'u smite [it] with flax,

---

[a] *Ḳaḳḳar balaṭi* occurs elsewhere in incantation fragments (K. 5,125, etc.). Cf. Jer. xi, 19.

[DIN]GIR-GU-NU-RA TARGUL-GAL-BI ḪU-MU-UN-DAR . .

^{ilu} „ *ina tar-gul-li-i ra-bi-tum lil-te-* . . . .

A-AN-AN-NA-UŠ-SA-GIM KI-A MU-UN-ŠI-IN-BAR-RA . . .

ki-ma zu-un-nu ša iš-tu šame(e) šur-du-u ana irṣitim(tim) uš-šu-[ru]

SU-BAR-RA-ZU-TA DINGIR-EN-KI LUGAL ZU-AB-GE ḪE-IM-MA-RA-AN-ZI-[ZI]

ina zu-um-[ri]-ka ^{ilu} *Ea šar ap-si-i li-is-suḫ-šu*

TE EN

EN ŠU-SAG (?) . . . . NAM-MULU-GIŠGAL-LU-GE

. . . *ri is* . . . *nu amelu tam-tim lim-nu*

kima labiri-šu šaṭir-ma bari u up-pu-uš duppi ^{m} *Iddina-* ^{ilu} *Bêl aplu ša*

. . . *-ziri mar* ^{m} *Mu-še-zib* . . *ḳatâ* ^{II} ^{m} ^{ilu} *Nergal* . . . *aplû-ša*

. . . . *-u-a*

May Gunura [strike (?) it] with a great oar (?).
Like rain which is let fall from heaven
Directed unto earth,
So may Ea, King of the Deep, remove it from thy body.
Exorcism, incantation.

INCANTATION OF THE PRAYER (?) . . . . OF MANKIND.

[Incantation :] . . . evil man of the sea (?)

[Colophon.]

Tablet of the Ban.

Tablet "V."

Obverse.

(Plate XXXIV.)

EN SAG-BA SAG-BA GIŠ-ḪAR-RA NU-BAL-E
ma - mit ma - mit u - ṣur - tu ša la e - te - ḳi
GIŠ - ḪAR DINGIR - RI - E - NE - GE NU - BAL - E
u - ṣu - rat ilâni^{pl} *ša la na - bal - ku - ti*
GIŠ - ḪAR ANA - KI - A NU - KUR - RU - DA
u-ṣu-rat šame(e) u irṣitim(tim) ša la ut-tak-ka-ru
DINGIR I - A - AN NU - BAL - E
ilu iš - ta - a - nu la muš - pi - lu
DINGIR-MULU-BA-GE NAM-MU-UN-DA-AN-BUR-RA
ilu u amelu la ip - pa - aš - ša - ru
GIŠ - PAR NU - DIB - BA ḪUL - IK - KU DA - A
giš-par-ru la e-ti-ḳu ša ana lim-ni ri-tu-u
SA - PAR NU - E - A ḪUL - IK - KU LAL - E
sa-pa-ru la a-ṣi-e ša ana lim-ni tar-ṣu
UTUG-ḪUL-ḪE-A A-LA-ḪUL-ḪE-A GIDIM-ḪUL-ḪE-A MULLA-ḪUL-ḪE-A DINGIR-ḪUL-ḪE-A MAŠKIM-ḪUL-ḪE-A
lu-u u-tuk-ku lim-nu lu-u a-lu-u lim-nu lu-u e-kim-mu lim-nu lu-u gal-lu-u lim-nu lu-u ilu lim-nu lu-u ra-bi-ṣu lim-nu
DINGIR-RAB-KAN-ME-ḪE-A DINGIR-RAB-KAN-ME-A-ḪE-A DINGIR-RAB-KAN-ME-KIL-ḪE-A
lu-u la-bar-tum lu-u la-ba-ṣu lu-u aḫ-ḫa-[zu]
MULU-LILLA-ḪE-A KI-EL-LILLA-ḪE-A KI-EL-UD-DA-KAR-RA-ḪE-A
lu-u li-lu-u lu-u li-li-tum lu-u ar-da-at li-[li-i]

Tablet of the Ban.

Tablet "V."

OBVERSE.

(PLATE XXXIV.)

Incantation :—

Ban! Ban! Barrier that none can pass,
Barrier of the gods, that none may break,
Barrier of heaven and earth that none can change,
Which no god may annul,
Nor god nor man can loose,
A snare without escape, set for evil,
A net whence none can issue forth, spread for evil,
Whether it be evil Spirit, or evil Demon, or evil Ghost,
Or evil Devil, or evil God, or evil Fiend,
Or Hag-demon, or Ghoul, or Robber-sprite,
Or Phantom, or Night-wraith, or Handmaid of the Phantom,

NAM - TAR - ḪUL - IK - ḪE - A [AZAG] - GIG - GA - ḪE - A
TUR - RA - NU - DUG - GA - ḪE - [A]

lu-u nam-ta-ru lim-nu lu-u a-šak-ku mar-ṣu lu-u mur-ṣu la ṭa-[a-bu]

A-SUR-RA DINGIR-EN-KI-GE SAG-BI IN-GA-GA-[E]

ša a-na me-e ṣar-ru-ti ša ^{ilu}E-a '-ir-[ru]

GIŠ-PAR DINGIR-EN-KI-GE KAN-NI-IB-DIB-[DIB-BI]

giš-par-ru ša ^{ilu}E-a li-bar-[ru]

KU-SUR-RA DINGIR-NIDABU-GE SAG-BI IB-TA-AN-BU-I

ša a-na ku-sur-ri-e ša ^{ilu}Ni-sa-ba i-ṣar-ru-ru

[SA]-PAR DINGIR-NIDABU-GE KAN-NI-IB-SAR-RI-E-NE

sa-pa-ru ša ^{ilu}Ni-sa-ba lik-su-šu

[GIŠ]-ḪAR-RA NI-BAL-E

u-ṣur-tum ib-ba-lak-ki-tu

GIŠ-ḪAR-RA GIŠ-ḪAR ANA-KI-A [1] ŠU-NAM-BA-BAR-RA

u-ṣur-ti ilâni ^{pl} u-ṣu-rat šame(e) u irṣitim(tim) a-a u-maš-šir-šu

ZI DINGIR-GAL-GAL-E-NE-GE IM-BA [2] -RA-NU-TUK-A

ša niš ilâni ^{pl} rabûti ^{pl} la i-pal-la-ḫu

ZI DINGIR-GAL-GAL-E-NE-GE SA [3] -ḪE-EN-DA [4]

niš ilâni ^{pl} rabûti ^{pl} li-ik-su-šu [5]

DINGIR-GAL-GAL-E-NE-GE NAM-ḪA-BA-RA [6] -TAR-RU-DA [7]

ilâni ^{pl} rabûti ^{pl} li-ru-ru-šu

(Plate XXXV.)

E-A-AN [8] GE-GE-E [9] -A

ša a-na bi-ti [10] *it-ta-nu-ur-ru*

E-SAG-GA-NA [11] KAN-NI-IB-TU-TU-NE

a-na [12] *bi-ti pi-ḫi-e* [13] *li-še-ri-bu-šu*

BAR-RA [14] NIGIN-E : *ša ina a-ḫa-a-ti* [15] *is-sa* [16] *-na-aḫ-ḫu-ru*

BAR-RA KI-BA [17] -RA [18] -LAL-E KAN-NI-IB-DU-MU-NE

ina [19] *a-ḫa-a-ti* [15] *a-šar la a* [20] *-ri li-ru-šu*

Or evil Plague, or Fever sickness, or unclean Disease,
Which hath attacked the shining waters of Ea.
May the snare of Ea catch it ;
Or which hath assailed the bonds of Nisaba,
May the net of Nisaba entrap it ;
Or which hath broken the barrier,
Let not the barrier of the gods,
The barrier of heaven and earth, let it go free !
Or which reverenceth not the great gods,
May the great gods entrap it ;
May the great gods curse it.

(PLATE XXXV.)

Or which attacketh the house,
Into a closed dwelling may they cause it to enter ;
Or which circleth round about,
Into a place without escape may they bring it.

---

[1] 93,082, GE.
[2] 93,082, BAR.
[3] D.T. 38, DI (= SA) ; 93,082, DI-DI (= SA-SA).
[4] D.T. 38, KA ; 93,082, DE.
[5] D.T. 38, [*lik*]-*šu-us-su* ; 93,082, *lik-ku-ut-su.*
[6] D.T. 38 and 93,082, DA-AN.
[7] D.T. 38, DE.
[8] 93,082, NI.
[9] D.T. 38 omits.
[10] D.T. 38, *ana bîti.*
[11] D.T. 38, GA-A-TA for GA-NA.
[12] D.T. 38, *ana.*
[13] D.T. 38, *i.*
[14] D.T. 38 inserts A-AN.
[15] D.T. 38, *tu.*
[16] D.T. 38, *ṣa.*
[17] D.T. 38, BAR.
[18] 93,083 inserts NI.
[19] D.T. 38, *a-na.*
[20] D.T. 38 and 93,083 insert *ma.*

KA - E - A[1] AN - GE - GE[2] - E - A
ša ina ba-ab[3] bi-ti[4] it-ta-nak-lu-u
E - KI - NU[5] - TA - E KAN - NI - IB - TU - TU - NE
a-na bi-ti[6] a-šar la a-ṣi-e[7] li-še-ri-bu-šu
GIŠ-GAL GIŠ-SAK-KUL-TA MU-UN-DA-AN- * GIR-
* GIR-RI-E-A
ša ina dal-ti u šik-ku-ri[8] i-ḫal-lu-pu[9]
GIŠ - GAL GIŠ - SAK - KUL - TA SA - NU - GAB - U - DA
KAN-NI-IB-SAR-RI-E-NE
dal-tu[10] u šik-ku-ru mar-kas la pa-ṭa-ri lik-lu-šu
I - LU - GIŠ - ZA - RA - TA MU - UN - ZA - LA - AḪ[11] - E - NE
ša ina as-kup-pa-ti u ṣir[12]-ri i-zik-ḳu[13]
GIŠ-KA-NA GIŠ-NU-SUR-U-TA[14] MU-UN[15]-SUR-
SUR-E-NE[16]
ša ina [iṣu] ka-nak-ki[17] nu-ku-še-e i-ṣar-ru-ru[18]
A-GIM ḪE-EN-BAL-E : *ki-ma me-e lit-bu-ku-šu*
DUG-GIM ḪE-EN-GAZ-E-NE : *ki-ma kar-pa-ti li-iḫ-pu-šu*
LA - GIM ḪE - EN - ŠU - UŠ - RI - E - [NE]
ki - ma ḫa - aṣ - bi li - par - ri - ru - šu
* UR-RA NI-BAL-E : *ša u-ru ib-ba-lak-[ki-tu]*
PA - BI KAN - NI - IB - TAR - RU
gap - pi - šu li - gaz - zi - [zu]
AB-TA TIG-BA-RA-LAL-E : *ša ina ap-ti [it-te-ni-'-lu]*
TIG-BI KAN-NI-IB-ŠUM-MU-NE : *ki-šad-su liṭ-bu-ḫu*
AB - TI - TA IGI - MU - UN - IN - BAR - RI - E - NE
ša ina ap - ti ṣi - li ip - pa - la - sa
IGI - BI ḪE - EN - SIG - GA - E - NE
pa - ni - šu lim - ḫa - ṣu
AB - ŠI - LA - TA GU - MU - UN - NA - AN - DE - E
ša ina ap - ti [ ] i - šis - si

Or which is shut in by the house-door,
Into a house without exit may they cause it to enter ;
Or that which passeth door and bolt,
With door and bolt, a bar immoveable, may they withhold it.
Or which bloweth in at the threshold and hinge,
Or which forceth a way through bar and latch.[a]
Like water may they pour it out,
Like a goblet may they dash it in pieces ;
Like a tile may they break it,
Or which passeth over the wall,
Its wing may they cut off ;
Or which [lieth] in a chamber,
Its throat may they cut ;
Or which looketh in at a side chamber,
Its face may they smite ;
Or which muttereth in a . . . chamber,

---

1 D.T. 38 reads KA-NA-A (*ša ina babi-šu*), i.e. "door" simply; 93,083, KA-DE-A.

2 D.T. 38, MAL-MAL (i.e. GA-GA).

3 D.T. 38, *bi.*

4 D.T. 38, *šu* ; 93,083, *bîti.*

5 D.T. 38 inserts *um.*

6 93,083 and D.T. 38, *ana bîti.*

7 93,083, *i.*

8 93,083, *ru.*

9 D.T. 38, *pa.*

10 D.T. 38, *da-al-tum,* omitting *u.*

11 D.T. 38 inserts ḪI.

12 D.T. 38, *ṣar.*

13 D.T. 38, *ḳa.*

14 D.T. 38 adds A-AN.

15 D.T. 38 omits MU-UN.

16 D.T. 38, A.

17 D.T. 38 inserts *u.*

18 D.T. 38, *ra.*

a *iṣu kanakku* and *iṣu nukušû* are both parts of a door, but what exactly is uncertain.

KA-BI ḪE-EN-TAB[1]-E-NE : *pa-a-šu li-di-lu*
AB-SAG-GA-TA MU-UN-DA-AB-ŠU-ŠU-NE
ša ina ap-ti muḫ-ḫi it-ta-na-at-ba-ku
GAKKUL-NU-BAD-DA-TA KAN-NI-IB-ŠU-ŠU-NE
kak-kul-ti la pa-te-e li-ik-tum-šu
LAḪ-TA[2] MU-UN-ŠI-IB-GIG-GIG-GA
ša ina na-ma-ri i-te-ni-ik-ki-la

(Plate XXXVI.)

LAḪ-TA KI DINGIR-BABBAR-E KAN-NI-IB-ZI-ZI-NE
ina na-ma-ri a-šar ṣi-it ^ilu^ *Šamši(ši) li-is-su-ḫu-šu*
GUL-GUL . . . . GIR-GIR-RI-E-NE
ša . . . . *bir-ḳi it-ta-nab-ri-ḳa*
GUL-GUL . . . . KAN-NI-IB-SAR-RI-E-NE
. . . . *lik-lu-šu*
. . . . MU-UN-ŠI-IB-KU-DU-NE
. . . . [KAN]-NI-IB-ŠUB-BU-NE
. . . . DA-*GIR-*GIR-RI-E-A
. . . . [KAN-NI]-IB-ŠUB-BU-NE
. . . . DA-AB-SA-SA-NE
. . . .

---

[1] K. 4,667, NI-IB . . . . for EN-TAB.
[2] D.T. 38, GA.

Its mouth may they shut ;
Or which roameth loose in an upper chamber,
With a bason[a] without opening may they cover it ;
Or which at dawn is darkened,

(PLATE XXXVI.)

At dawn to a place of sunrise may they take it ;
Or which . . . with the lightning flasheth,
. . . . . . may they enclose it ;
[Or which] . . . . . . chirpeth,
. . . . may they smite it ;
[Or which] . . . . . passeth through,
. . . . may they smite it,
. . . .

---

[a] *Kakkultu*, the equivalent of the same ideogram as *namzitu*, a metal vessel quoted in lists of spoil and in contract-tablets. The Syriac *kâkôltâ* means "a cake" (Brockelmann, *Lexicon*, p. 157*a*), and if the two words are to be connected *kakkultu* will probably mean a flattish vessel of some kind. Here it is evidently meant to be turned upside down to enclose the evil influence.

Tablet of an Evil Spirit.

Tablet "X."

[Obverse wanting.]

REVERSE.

(PLATE XXXVI.)

. . . .

. . [UTUG-ḪUL-IK] . . . KUR-RA-NI KAS-KAS : „ *e-kim* . . . [*mut-taš-rab-bi-ṭu mâti*]

. . [UTUG-ḪUL-IK] KALAM-MA TU-GIM KU-KU : „ *ša ma-a-tu ki-ma* [*ṣu-ba-ti u-lab-bi-iš*]

. . [UTUG-ḪUL-IK] MULU-RA KA-ḪUŠ . . . : „ *ša eli ameli iz-z*[*i*] . . .

5. . . [UTUG-ḪU]L-IK MULLA GIŠ-NU-TUK : „ *gal-lu-u la* [*še-mu-u*]

. . [UTUG]-ḪUL-IK MULLA UR-NU-TUK : „ *gal-lu-u* [*ša bul-ta la i-šu-u*]

. . [UTUG]-ḪUL-IK MULLA ŠU-ḪUL SA-A : „ *gal-lu-u ša lim-niš i-ri-iḫ-ḫu-u*

. . [UTUG]-ḪUL-IK KALAM-MA ZI-IR-ZI-IR : „ *ša ma-a-tu i-aš-ša-a-šu*

. . [UTUG-ḪU]L-IK KALAM-MA NIGIN-E : „ *ša ina ma-a-ti iṣ-ṣa-nun-du*

10. . . [UTUG-ḪUL]-IK KALAM-ZI-IK DIB-DIB BI : „ *ša ni-ši šik-na-at na-piš-ti ib-ta-na-'-rum*

. . [UTUG-ḪUL-IK] NAM-TAR ŠU ŠUR-RA : „ *nam-ta-ru ša ḳa-ta al-pu*

. . [UTUG-ḪUL-IK KALAM-MA] ḪUL-A NIGIN-NA : „ *ša ina ma-a-ti mit-ḫa-riš iṣ-ṣa-nun-du*

. . [UTUG-ḪUL-IK KALAM-MA Ḫ]UL-A LU-LU-A : „ *ša ina ma-a-ti mit-ḫa-riš id-dal-la-ḫu*

Tablet of an Evil Spirit.

Tablet "X."

Reverse.

(Plate XXXVI.)

The evil Spirit robbeth . . . and roameth over the land,

The evil Spirit which shroudeth the land as with a garment,

The evil Spirit which against the man angrily . . .

The evil Spirit is a devil which heareth not,

The evil Spirit is a devil which hath no shame,

The evil Spirit is a devil which spawneth evilly,

The evil Spirit which bringeth woe on the land,

The evil Spirit which hunteth over the land,

The evil Spirit which chaseth living beings,

The evil Spirit is a Pestilence which . . . (?) the hand,

The evil Spirit which fiercely hunteth the land,

The evil Spirit which fiercely raiseth trouble in the land,

. . [UTUG-ḪUL-IK] . . . NU-BU-I : „ *ša* . . . *la i-maḫ-ḫa-ru*

. . . [UTUG-ḪUL-IK TUR-TUR-RA ḪA-GIM]A BA-AN-SU: „ *ša ṣi-iḫ-ḫi-ru-ti ki-ma nu-ni ina me-e i-šaḫ-ḫa-lum*

. . [UTUG-ḪUL-IK GAL-GAL-LA] . . . RU-RU : „ *ša rab-bu-tim ma-ag-ra-niš it-ta-nam-du-u*

. . [UTUG-ḪUL-IK] . . . TUN-TUN : „ *ša ši-ba u šip-ta i-ḫat-tu-u*

. . [UTUG-ḪUL-IK SILA] . . : „ *ša su-ḳa in-* . . .

. . [UTUG-ḪUL-IK . . . . . : „] *ša* . . . . .

. . . .

The evil Spirit which receiveth not . . . .

15. The evil Spirit which draweth up the little ones like fish from the water,

The evil Spirit which casteth down the elders . .

The evil Spirit which striketh greyhaired old men and women,

The evil Spirit which . . . . . . the street,

[The evil Spirit] which . . . .

. . . .

𝔗𝔞𝔟𝔩𝔢𝔱 "𝔙."

OBVERSE.

(PLATE XXXVII.)[1]

EN DINGIṚ-DIB-DIB-BI-E-NE URUGAL-LA-[TA]
IM - TA - E - A - [MEŠ]
ilâni^{pl} *ka-mu-ti iš-tu ḳab-rim it-ta-ṣu-ni*
MULLA - E - NE - ḪUL - A - MEŠ URUGAL - LA - TA
IM - TA - E - A - MEŠ
za-ḳi-ḳu lim-nu-ti iš-tu ḳab-rim it-ta-ṣu-ni
KI - * SIG - GA - A - DE - A - AN URUGAL - LA - TA
IM - TA - E - A - MEŠ
a-na ka-sa-ap ki-is-pi u na-aḳ mi-e
iš - tu ḳab - rim „
GAR - ḪUL - IK - E . . *VII* - NA - NE - NE
A - MA - RU - GIM MU - UN - ZI - ZI
mimma lim - nu [*ina*] *kiš - šat - su - nu*
ki - ma a - [*bu*] - *ba it - te - bu - ni*
IB-BA-A-NI MI-NI-[IN-Z]I-ZI . . . ŠU-ḪA-BA-AB
NU - MU - UN . . . .
ag - giš te - bu - [*u - ni*] . . . . . .
ZI - GA - BI . . . .
. . . .

---

[1] Col. V, Reverse, contains the following beginnings of lines :—(1) ZI . . . (2) . . . (3) *niš* ^{ilu} . . . (4) *mu-du* . . . (5) ZI DINGIR-SIS-[KI] . . . (6) EN-M[IR] . . . (7) *niš* ^{ilu} *Sin ta* . . . (8) *be-el a-*[*gi-e*] . . . (9) *niš* ^{ilu} . . .

Tablet "V."

OBVERSE.

(PLATE XXXVII.)

The gods which seize upon man
Have gone forth from the grave,
The evil windblasts
Have gone forth from the grave,
To demand the paying of rites and the pouring of libations
They have gone forth from the grave,
All that is evil in their hosts like a whirlwind
Hath gone forth from the grave,
Angrily they come . . . .
. . . .

Tablet "BB."

(Plate XL.)

EN AZAG . . . BI MULU-RA MU-UN-NA-SUR
EME-NI EME NIM-GIR-A-AN MULU-RA MU-UN-NA-SUR
TUR-RA SAG-GIG ŠA-GIG LIKIR-GIG-GA-A-AN
UḪ PU LAL TAR-RI SIR UG PA-AG
MU-UN-DA-AB-ZA
UḪ (?) BAR-BAR-RA-BI A-GIM LUḪ-LUḪ-ḪA
ŠI LAM TIG UN RI IDIM A-AB-BA ŠAR-ŠAR
TIG GAR-GAR-RA-BI IM-MA-NI-IN-ŠAR-ŠAR
GIŠ-GIG-GIM IM-TA-U-TU-UD-DA
ID-SA-PAR-GIM MULU MU-UN-ŠI-IN-TE-MAL
GIŠ-EŠ-ŠUR-RA-BI SU-LU-UG
MU-UN-[DA]-AB-ZA
GIŠ-GAR-LAL KUD-DA BI . . . .
ŠI . . . .
. . . MULU ŠAR . . . .
. . . .

Tablet "BB."

(Plate XL.)

Incantation :—

Fever which . . . against the man flasheth,
Its tongue flasheth against the man as a tongue of lightning,
Sickness, Headache, Heart disease, Heartache.
. . . .
. . . .
Venom like water foameth at his jaws,
. . . . . . in the bed of Ocean hath mingled,
. . . . . . his . . . hath mingled,
Like a shadow it is born
Like a net it hath drawn nigh unto the man.
. . . .
. . . .

Tablet "CC."

Obverse.

(Plate XLI.)

EN UTUG-ḪUL A-LA-ḪUL GIDIM-ḪUL MULLA-ḪUL
E-KI-KUR-TA TI A . . . .

u-tuk-ku lim-nu a-lu-u lim-nu e-kim-mu lim-nu
gal-lu-u lim-nu ul-tu ir-ṣi-tu it-ta-ṣu-nu šu-nu

ŠU KUR - TI - TA - ŠA - BI IM - TI - A - MEŠ

iš-tu KU-AZAG *ana ki-rib mâtim(tim)*
it-ta-ṣu-nu šu-nu

ANA NU - ZU - MEŠ KI - A NU - ZU - MEŠ

ina šame(e) ul it-ta-du-u ina irṣitim(tim) ul il-la-mad

GUB-BA NU-UN-NU-ZU-MEŠ TUŠ NU-UN-NU-ZU-MEŠ

u - su - uz - zu ul i - du - u a - šab - ba ul i - du - u

U NU - UN - DA - AB - KU A NI - DE - AB - NAK

a - kal ul ik - kal mê^pl ul i - šat - tu

The Reverse bears the following inscription:—

A - na ^ilu^ Nabu sukkalli ṣi - i - ri
ša nap - ḫar par - ṣi ḫa - am - mu
a - ša - rid . . . da - a . . . .
ša e - lu . . . .

Tablet "CC."

OBVERSE.

(PLATE XLI.)

Incantation :—

The evil Spirit, the evil Demon, the evil Ghost, the evil Devil,
From the earth have come forth ;
From the Underworld (?) unto the land they have come forth,
In heaven they are unknown,
On earth they are not understood,
They know not how to stand,
They know not how to sit,
No food they eat,
No water they drink.

The Reverse states that the tablet was a votive offering to Nabu, and it was doubtless intended to be placed in the Library in the Temple of that god in Nineveh.

Series Luḫ-ka.

The Eighth Tablet.

OBVERSE.

(PLATE XLI.)[1]

[EN E-SIR-RA DU]-A-NI-TA : *su-ga-am ina a-la-ki-šu*

. . . . . ŠAR (?) E-SIR-RA DU-A-NI-TA

. . . . . . *su-ga-am ina a-la-ki-šu*

[SILA-DAGAL]-LA DIB-BA-A-NI-TA : *ri-bi-tu ina ba-'-i-šu*

[E-SIR-RA] SILA-A GIN-NA-A-NI-TA : *su-u-ḳa su-la-a ina a-la-ki-šu*

[ŠU]-*NAG-A-BAL-E-DA MU-UN-DA-GUG-MA

ri-im-ka tab-ka ik-bu-us-ma

A-SI-NU-SA-A GIR-NI BA-NI-IN-GAR

ina me-e la i-ša-ru-ti še-ip-šu iš-ta-ka-an

A-ŠU-NU-LUḪ-ḪA IGI-IM-MA-AN-SUM : *me-e ḳa-ti la mi-sa-a-ti i-ta-mar*

SAL ŠU-NU-*ŠIG-GA GAB-IM-MA-AN-RI

sin-niš-tu ša ḳa-ta-ša la dam-ḳa uš-tam-ḫi-ir

KI-EL ŠU-NU-LUḪ-ḪA IGI-IM-MA-AN-SUM

ar-da-tu ša ḳa-ta-ša la mi-sa-a it-tap-la-as

Series Luḫ-ka.

The Eighth Tablet.

OBVERSE.

(PLATE XLI.)

[a][Incantation :—]
While he walked in the street,
. . . while he walked in the street,
While he made his way through the broad places,
While he walked along the streets and ways,
He trod in some libation that had been poured forth, or
He put his foot in some unclean water,
Or cast his eye on the water of unwashen hands,
Or came in contact with a woman of unclean hands,
Or glanced at a maid with unwashen hands,

---

[1] Of Tablet VII of this series only the last line is left (see Plate XL):—

li - ša - nu li - mut - tu ina a - ḫa - [a - ti li - iz - ziz]

INIM - INIM - MA ERI - A AZAG . . . .

EN E - SIR - RA DU - A - [NI - TA]

Duppi VII KAM-MA LUḪ - KA

[a] Tablet "AA" is a continuation of Tablet VIII of this series.

[SAL] UḪ(?)-RI-A ŠU MU-NI-IN-TAG : *sin-niš-tu ša ru-ḫi-e ḳat-su il-ta-pat*
[MULU ŠU]-NI-NU-*ŠIG-GA GAB-IM-MA-AN-RI
[*ša ḳa*]-*ta-šu la dam-ḳu uš-tam-ḫi-ir*

TABLET "AA."

(PLATE XXXVIII.)

[MULU ŠU-NI-NU-LUḪ-ḪA] IGI-[IM-MA-AN-SUM]
ša ḳa-[*ta-šu*] *la mi*-[*sa-a-ti i-ta-mar*]
MULU SU-NA SI-NU-[SA-A] ŠU-MU-NI-[IN-TAG]
ša zu-mur-šu la i-ša-ru ḳat-su il-ta-[*pat*]
DINGIR-SILIG-MULU-ŠAR [IGI-IM-MA]-AN-SUM
ilu Marduk ip-pal-li-is-su-[*ma*]
A-A-NI DINGIR-EN-KI-RA ID-RA-GE ŠU-A-BA-AN-NA-GI . . .
a-na ilu E-a a-bi-šu ina ap-si-i u-ša-an-na
A-A-MU MAS-MAS A ŠU-*ELTEG-A-BAL-E-NE[1]
MU-UN-DA-GUG-MA MU-UN-DA-GUG-MA
a-bi maš-maš-šu ri-im-ka tab-ka ik-bu-us ik-bu-us-ma
A-SI-NU-SA[2]-A GIR-NI BA-NI-IN-GAR
ina me-e la i-ša-ru-ti še-ip-šu iš-ta-ka-an
A-ŠU NU-LUḪ-ḪA IGI-IM-MA-AN-SUM
[3]SAL ŠU-NU-*ŠIG-GA GAB-IM-MA-AN-RI
KI-EL ŠU-NU-LUḪ-ḪA IGI-IM-MA-AN-SUM
SAL *UḪ-RI-A ŠU-MU-NI-IN-TAG
MULU ŠU-NI[4]-NU-*ŠIG-GA GAB-IM-MA-AN-RI
MULU ŠU-NI[5]-NU-LUḪ-ḪA IGI-IM-MA-AN-SUM

Or his hand touched a bewitched woman,
Or he came in contact with a man of unclean hands,

TABLET "AA."

(PLATE XXXVIII.)

Or saw one with unwashen hands,
Or his hand touched one of unclean body.
Marduk hath seen him, and
Unto Ea his father in the Deep told it:
"Father, his magician in some poured out libation hath trodden, hath trodden, or
"He hath put his foot in some unclean water,
"Or he hath cast his eye on the water of unwashen hands,
"Or he hath come in contact with a woman of unclean hands,
"Or he hath glanced at a maid with unwashen hands,
"Or his hand hath touched a bewitched woman,
"Or he hath come in contact with a man of unclean hands,
"Or he hath seen one with unwashen hands,

---

[1] K. 4,900, DA. [2] S. 924, SI.
[3] K. 4,900 and K. 6,029 translate *me-e ḳa-ti la mi-sa-a-ti i-ta-mar.*
[4] S. 924 omits. [5] S. 924 and K. 6,029 omit.

MULU SU-NI[1] SI-NU-SA-A ŠU-MU-NI-IN-TAG
ša zu-mur-šu la i-ša-ru il-ta-[pat]
A-NA IB-BA-ŠA-A[2]-EN[3] GA-E BA[4]-DA-LAL-E
mi-nam te-ib-bi-eš[5] *ia-a*[6]*-ši*[7] *kul-li-man-ni*
DINGIR-EN-KI-GE[8] DU-A[9]-NI DINGIR-SILIG-MULU-ŠAR MU-UN-NA-NI-IB-GE-GE
^{ilu}*E-a mâri-šu* ^{ilu}*Marduk ip-[pal]*
DU-MU A-NA NU-E[10]-ZU A-NA-A RA-AB-DAḪ
[DINGIR-SILIG]-MULU-ŠAR A-NA NU-NI-ZU A-NA-A RA-AB-DAḪ
GAR-GA-E NI-ZU-A-MU-U ZA-E IN-GA-E
GIN-NA DU-MU DINGIR-SILIG-MULU-[ŠAR]
[DUG]-SAR-RA GAR(?) UDUN-GAL-TA GIN-A ŠU-U-ME-[TI]
ša kar-pa-tu ša-ḫar-ra-tu ša ul-tu u-tu-ni ra-bi-tu
[il-la-ḳu] li-ḳi-e-[ma]
ID KA-*II*-ṆA-TA A-ŠU A U-ME-NI- . .
ina pi-i na-[ra-a-ti ki]-lal-li me-e sa-am-ma
GIŠ-ŠINIG U-IN-NU-UŠ GIŠIMMAR-DU GI-SUL-ŠAR
[* ELTEG SI MUN KA-BAR-RA ?] DINGIR-RI-E-NE-GE
bi-i-nu [maš-ta]-kal su-ḫuš-ša ḳa-an ša-la-la
u-ḫu-la ḳar-na-nu [ṭa]-ab-tu pi-ta-a-at pi-i i-li
. . . . BA-LAM GIŠ-KU RIG-ZUN RIG-LI RIG-LU-LU GIŠ-ERIN-BABBAR-RA
. . . . *su-pa-lu ur-ḳa-rin-na ri-ḳi bu-ra-ši ku-dur-ru li-ia-ru*

---

[1] S. 924, NA; K. 4,900 and K. 6,029, BI.

[2] S. 924, GE for ŠA-A.

[3] K. 4,900, K. 6,029, and S. 924 omit.

[4] S. 924 and K. 4,900 insert AN.

[5] S. 924, *pu-uš* for *bi-eš*.

"Or his hand hath touched one of unclean body;
"Show unto me what thou wouldst do."
Ea hath answered his son Marduk:
"O my son, what dost thou not know?
"What more can I give thee?
"O Marduk, what dost thou not know?
"What can I add unto thy knowledge?
"What I know thou knowest also.
"Go, my son Marduk,
"Take an earthen vessel
"Which hath come from a great kiln, and
"At the confluence of two streams bale up[a] water and
"*Bînu*, the *maštakal*-plant, *suḫuššu*, a stalk of *šalalu*,[b]
The "horned alkali,[c]" salt that openeth the mouth of the gods,
. . . *supalu*, *urkarinnu*, (?), cypress, *kudurru*, *liaru*,

[6] S. 924 omits.
[7] K. 4,900, *ti*.
[8] K. 6,029 omits.
[9] S. 924 and K. 6,029 omit.
[10] K. 4,900 and K. 6,029, NI.

[a] *Samma* (= *sab-ma* ?), meaning uncertain.

[b] On *šalalu* see p. 107.

[c] *Uḫulu*, according to Delitzsch, *H.W.B.*, p. 43*b*, means alkali, the same word as the Syriac *aḫlâ*. It is described in Payne Smith, 125, as "'*herba quae detergendae cuti teritur in pulvere.*' Ferr."

(PLATE XXXIX.)

. . . [GIŠ-ERIN] BUR NI SAG NI RIG DINGIR NIN-IB
. . . . . * LAL UD . . . . . DU - A
. . [*e*]-*ri-nu* [*šamnu*[1] *e*]*l-la*[2] *šamnu*[1] *ru-uš-tu*[3] *šamnu*[1] *ni-kib-ti*
. . . . . *ana šadi - šu ib - bab - la*
. . . . . NI LID ŠILAM-AZAG-GA-TA SAR . . .
. . . . . *el - li - ti ša - man ar - ḫi*
ša ina tar - ba - ṣi el - [*li*][2] *ib - ba - nu* - [*u*]
. . . GE TAK-GAB-ŠI-A TAK-NINI-ŠI TAK-NINI-MUŠ-GIR TAK . . .
. . . . GUG TAK - ZAGIN - NA
. . . *ṣa-ri-ri du-ša-a muš-gar-ru ḫu-la-la sa-an-tu*[4] *uk-na-a*

REVERSE.

ŠA - A - GUB - BA - KU U - ME - NI - ŠUB
ana lib a - gub - bi - e i[5] *- di - ma*
. . . . . [E]L-LA NUN-KI-GA-GE U-ME-NI-GUB
. . . *el - la ša* ^{alu}*Eridi ki - in - ma*
. . . . . . ZU - AB - TA U - ME - NI - ŠA
. . . . . . *ap - si - i e - pu - uš - ma*
[NAM - ŠUB - DUG] - GA - ZU U - ME - NI - ŠUB[6]
ši - pat - ka ṭa - ab - [*ta*] *i - di - ma*
[A - NE NAM - ŠIB - BA - TA] U - ME - NI - DU
me - e - šu - nu - ti ina i - šip - pu - ti šuk - lil - ma
[NAM - ŠUB - EL - LA - ZU - TA] U - ME - NI - RI
ina ši - ip - ti - ka el - li - ti ul - lil - ma
[GIŠ (?) -BA-AN-GAB]-GAB-ID-LAL-E GIŠ-GAM-MA ŠU-U-ME-TI
[„ - *e* ^{iṣu}*kip - pa - ti*] *li - ḳi - ma*

(PLATE XXXIX.)

. . . cedar, pure oil, oil of balsam (?),[a] oil of *nikibti*.

honey . . . . (which) hath been brought down from the hills,

Pure . . . . (and) the fat of a cow

Which hath been made in a clean sheepfold.

. . . *ṣariru*-metal, *dusû*-stone, *mušgarru*-stone, *ḫulalu*-stone, *santu*-stone, *uknu*-stone,

REVERSE.

Place in a laver and

Arrange the pure . . . of Eridu and

Make the . . . of the Deep and

Perform thy goodly Incantation and

Make perfect the waters thereof with priestcraft and

With thy pure Incantation do thou cleanse (him) and

Take a bundle of twigs (?),

---

[1] K. 4.900, *šam-nu*. [2] K. 4,900, *ellu*.
[3] K. 4,900, *ti*. [4] K. 4,900, *du*.
[5] K. 4,900, *id*. [6] K. 4,900, SUM.

[a] *Ruštu*, perhaps the Chaldee *rîḫûš* (Levy, 420, *a*).

. . . . . . BA - A U - ME - NI - DE
[me] - e - šu - nu - ti ana lib - bi šu - puk - ma
[A - GUB] - BA E - DINGIR - RI - E - NE AZAG - GI - NE
a - gub - ba mu - ul[1] *- lil bit i - li*
[A - GU]B - BA E - DINGIR - RI - E - NE EL - E - NE
a - gub - bu - u mu - ub[1] *- bi - ib* [„]
A-GUB-BA E-DINGIR-RI-E-NE LAḪ-LAḪ-GI-[NE]
[a - gub - bu - u] mu - nam - mir[2] [„]
A - GUB - BA GU - LAḪ - ḪA DINGIR - RI - E - NE
a - gub - ba - a mi - is pi - e[3] *ša ilâni*^{pl}
A - GUB - BA ERI - A AZAG - GI[4] - E - NE
A - GUB - BA ERI - A EL - LA - E - NE

(PLATE XL.)

A - GUB - BA ERI SUN - SUN - NA[5] - E - NE
ŠU - U - ME - TI ERI - A U - ME - NI - [E]
li - ḳi - e - ma alu šu - bi - ' - [šu]
SILA - DAGAL - LA ERI - A U - ME - NI - [E]
ri - bit ali šu - bi - ' - [šu]
DINGIR - AŠ - A - AN . . . SIG - GA - BI U - ME - NI - [E]
. . . . . . *ḳa - ḳa - a šu - bi - ' - [šu]*
. . . . BI - KU U - ME - NI - [E]
. . . . *ru šu - bi - ' - [šu]*
. . . . A (?) GU . . .
. . . . *sa - a mas* . . .
. . . . : *a*
. . . .

[1] K. 4,900 omits.
[2] K. 4,813 . . . . *ir*.
[3] K. 4,813, *i*.
[4] S. 924, GA.
[5] S. 924 omits.

Pour the waters thereof on it and
The laver which cleanseth the Temple of the Gods,
The laver which purifieth the Temple of the Gods,
The laver which maketh bright the Temple of the Gods,
The laver which washeth the mouth of the Gods,
The laver which cleanseth the city,
The laver which purifieth the city,

(Plate XL.)

The laver[a] which maketh bright the city,
Take thou and bring to the city,
Bring to the broad place of the city,
Bring . . . .
Bring . . . .
. . . .

[a] It is possible that *agubbû* has the meaning of "pure water" all through this incantation.

Descriptions of Gods, etc.

Tablet "DD."

OBVERSE.

COL. II (PLATE XLII).

. . . .

ḳakḳadu [*ku - u*]*b - šu u ḳarnu* . . . . *- tum*
bur - ṣa - ṣa [*šaknat*](*at*) *lam - ṣa - ti šaknat*(*at*)
ap - pa - ri - tu šaknat(*at*) *rit - ta ša ameli*
sip - pu - ra rak - sa - at
irat - sa pi - ta - a - at
ina šumeli-ša še-ir-ra na-šat-ma ṣirti-ša ik-kal
ina imitti - ša i - ḳar - rab
iš - tu ḳakḳadi - ša ana sip - pu - ri - ša
pa - ag - ru sinništu me - ri - nu

---

[a] *Burṣaṣu* is the Chaldee *barṣuṣ*, part of the headdress worn by the priests (Exod. xxxix, 28), Levy, *Chald. Wörterb.*, 117, *a.* Bezold reads *-gar* (?)*-za-za* (*Z.A.* ix, 118) and *pur-za-za* (?), l. 76 (*Z.A.* ix, 407).

[b] *Lamṣatu* has the meaning of a kind of fly, but whether this holds good here it is difficult to say.

[c] *Apparritu* is to be connected with the Heb. *ᵃphêr*, a headdress with which a prophet (1 Kings xx, 38, 41) disguises himself. He is able to reveal himself by removing it from his face. In l. 20 the *apparritu* is worn *ina liti*, i.e. in (or on) the *litu*, which is also probably a headdress (see ll. 76, 92) and is to be compared to the

Descriptions of Gods, etc.

Tablet "DD."

OBVERSE.

COL. II (PLATE XLII).

. . . .

The head (has) a fillet and a horn . . .
She wears a head-ornament,[a] she wears a fly (?).[b]
She wears a veil[c]; the fist of a man;
She is girt about the loins[d];
Her breast is open,
In her left arm she holds a babe sucking her breast.
Inclining towards her right arm;
From her head to her loins
The body is that of a naked woman[e];

Hebrew *liwyâh*, "crown" or "wreath" (Prov. i, 9; iv, 9). As is sometimes to be seen in the terra-cotta figures of the goddess, who is represented holding a babe in her left arm, a long veil covers the back part of the headdress and falls down the back.

[d] *Sippuru* from this line and l. 9 ("from her head to her *sippuri*") evidently means "loins" or something similar, as Bezold has pointed out.

[e] *Sinništu merinu*, from the root *erû*, "to be naked."

iš - tu sip - pu - ri - ša ana ka - an ṭap - pi - ša
ku - li - ip - tu kima ṣiri a - ta - at
pa - pa - an libbi - ša a - gi - i i - ta - ad - du
šum - šu ^{ilu}NIN - TU *šu - ut* ^{ilu}MAḪ

ḳaḳḳadu ḳaḳḳad ṣiri
ina ap - pi - šu ḫi - in - zu uz - zu - ru
ina pi - šu mu - u šu - gal - lu - lu - ni
[uznâ] $^{II\ pl}$ *ki - ma ba - aš - mi ša - kin*
[ḳarnâ ^{II}*]* ^{pl}*-šu a-na III-šu un-ḳa-a-ti i-ta-ad-da-a*
[a]p - par - ri - tu ina li - ti - šu ša - kin
[p]ag - ru SUḪ - ḪA *kakkabâni* ^{pl} *ma - li*
[libit] šepi ^{pl} *- šu zu - up - ra ši - na*

REVERSE.

COL. III.

ka - an ṭap - pu - ša iḳ - ba la iši
šum - šu Sa - as - su u - ri (?) *- in - nu*
la - aḫ - mi tamti šu - [ut] ^{ilu}*E - a*

---

[a] *Kan ṭappî*, from the expression in this line "from the loins to her *kan ṭappî*," evidently signifies some part of the feet, and hence *ṭappû* must undoubtedly be referred to the Hebrew *ṭephaḫ*, "the palm of the hand," i.e., the sole of the foot. *Kannu* is the same as ṭhe Hebrew *kên*, the Syriac *kanna* (Brockelmann, p. 160, *b*), "basis."

[b] *Kuliptu* from its connection is probably the same as the Syriac *ḳ'laph'tha*, squama (Brockelmann, p. 324, *a*), in spite of the change from *k* to *ḳ*.

[c] *Papan libbi* is uncertain, but "navel" seems a probable translation. Bezold, "das Pochen (?) ihres Herzens bewegt (?) die Meeresflut" (*Z.A.* ix, 116).

From the loins to the sole of the foot [a]
Scales [b] like those of a snake are visible.
Her navel [c] is composed of a circlet;
Her name is Nin-tu, a form of the Goddess Maḫ.[d]

The head is the head of a serpent;
From his nostrils mucus trickles,[e]
His mouth is beslavered with water;
The ears are like those of a basilisk,
His horns are twisted into three curls,
He wears a veil in his headband,[f]
The body is a *Suḫ*-fish [g] full of stars,
The base of his feet are claws,

REVERSE.

COL. III.

The sole of his foot has no heel [h];
His name is *Sassu-urinnu* (?),
A sea-monster, a form of Ea.

---

[d] *Nin-tu* and *Maḫ* are both forms of the goddess *Belit-ili*.

[e] *Uzzuru* probably to be referred to the Syriac *'zir*, involutus (Brockelmann, p. 247, *b*). *Ḫinzu* is doubtful.

[f] *Litu*, see note to l. 4.

[g] Bezold, *pir-ḫa*. The *Suḫ*-fish occurs, however, in the omen-texts (Boissier, *Documents Relatives*, p. 173, l. 29).

[h] *Iḳba*, Hebrew *'âḳêbh*.

ḳakḳadu ku-ub-šu ḫup-di—im-mu . . . -gu-u
ḳarnu ṣabiti (?) *ištat*(*at*) *ana ku-tal-li-ša ki-ra-at*
ḳarnu ṣabiti (?) *ištat*(*at*) *ana pa-ni-ša id-da-at*
uz-nu immeri rit-tum ameli
ina ki-la-te-ša a-ka-la na-šat-ma ana pî-ša u-rib
pa-gar-ša nûni ana ku-tal-li-ša kap-pat
kan ṭap-pa-ša . . . .
šar-tu iš-tu bi-rit ḳarnâti^{pl}*-ša*
ana ša-šal-li-ša na-da-[*at*]
it-ti kan ṭap-pi-ša il-ta-ma- . . .

(Plate XLIII.)

iš-tu ḳabli-ša a-di kan ṭap-pi-ša ka- . .
man-za-az ina lib-bi it-ta . . . .
a-gi-i i-[*ta-ad-du*]
ku-lip-ta kima [*ṣiri a-ta-at*]
šum-šu . . . .
u-tu-ti ^{ilu}NIN-KI-GAL . . . .

---

ku-bu-uš ḳakḳadi-[*šu*] . . . .
ḳaran alpi šakin(*in*) *šar-tum* [*iš-tu ḳarnâti*^{pl}*-šu*]
ana ša-šal-li-šu na-di . . . .
pa-nu ameli li-tum [*šakin*]

---

[a] Bezold reads *it-ra-at*; but both *kirat* and *iddat* are used of the shape of the moon's horns (see my *Reports*, Nos. 26, 30).

[b] *Kilate* has been compared to the Hebrew *kil'aim* and translated "both (hands)." (See Muss-Arnolt, *Dictionary*, p. 390, *b*.)

[c] Bezold reads (*Z.A.* ix, 118) *pa-gar-ša ha-diš ku-pi-li-ša kap-pat*, translating "ihren Körper schlägt sie lustig (*ḫadiš*) mit ihrem Schwanze."

The head (has) a fillet ; . . . .
One horn, that of a gazelle, bent over her back,
The other horn, that of a gazelle, straight[a] over her face.
The ear of a sheep, the fist of a man,
In her two hands (?)[b] she holds food which she puts into her mouth,
Her body is that of a fish[c] bent backwards,
The sole of her foot is . . . .
Hair lies from between her horns
As far as her shoulders (?),[d]
It . . . . with the sole of her foot.

(PLATE XLIII.)

From her middle to the sole of her foot is . . .
The position therein . . . . .
[Is made of] a circlet ;
Scales like those of [a snake are visible],
Her name is . . . .
The chosen of Ereshkigal.

The fillet of his head . . . .
He has the horn of an ox ; hair lies [from between the horns]
As far as his shoulders . . . .
The face of a man ; [he has] a headband ;

---

d *Šašalli* is evidently some part of the back. A veil, as well as hair, falls down to it (l. 114).

---

kap - pi šakin(in) šepâ^{II} *- šu maḫ - ra . . .*

pag - ru nêši ina IV šepâ^{II} *. . . . . . .*

šum - šu ^{ilu} *. . . . .*

ḳaḳḳadu ḳaḳḳad ki - is - [su - gi]

ḳu - ma - ar - šu ša imitti ša . . . .

si - si - it rit - ti ša . . . .

ri - it - ta - šu ša . . . .

ina ki - la - te - šu šame(e) [naši]

sip - pu - ra [ra - kis]

ina šepi - šu ša imitti ir - ṣi - ta [ša - pi - iṣ]

libit šepi - šu ša imitti ṣupur iṣṣuri . . .

šepi - šu ša šumeli tar - [ṣa - at - ma]

kin - za ša ṭap - pi - e - šu . . . .

pag - ru me - ri - nu . . . .

šum - šu A - . . . .

laḫ - mu šu - ut . . . .

Lower Part of Col. III.

. . . .

. . . šu . . . .

. . . ša - pi - iṣ sip - pu - ra [ra - kis]

[ina šepi - šu] ša šumeli ir - ṣi - ta ša - pi - iṣ

[šepi - šu] ša imitti šu - te - gu - rat - ma

[kin - za] ša ṭap - pi - šu ša - pi - iṣ

He has wings ; his feet are advancing . . .
The body of a lion with four legs . . .
His name is the god . . . .

The head is the head of a *kissugu* (?),
He wears an armlet (?)[a] on his right arm. . .
The fingers (?) of the hand are those of . . .
The fist is that of a . . . .
In his two hands (?) [he holds (?)] the heavens,
[He is girt about] the loins,
With his right foot [he touches (?)] the earth,
The base of his right foot is a bird's claw . .
His left foot is stretched out
The flat (?) of his footsole . . . .
The body is a naked . . . .
His name is A . . . .
A monster, a form of . . . .

LOWER PART OF COL. III.

. . . .
He touches (?) . . . [he is girt about] the waist,
With his left foot he touches (?) the earth,
His right foot . . . .
With the flat (?) of his sole he touches (?)

---

[a] *Ḳumar* may be connected with the Syriac *ḳamra*, cingulum, and *ḳumra*, vinculum (?), (Brockelmann, p. 326, *a-b*).

[*libit šepi-šu*] *ša imitti-šu zu-pur iṣṣuri-ma*
[*ḳin*] - *za sa ṭap - pi - šu - ma ša - pi - iṣ*

(PLATE XLIV.)

. . . *neši šakin(in) pag-ru me-ri-in-nu ki-is-su-gu*
[*šum*] - *šu La - aḫ - mu ip - pi - ru*
. . . *-nu-tum la-aḫ-mu sa šame(e) u irṣitim(tim)*
[*laḫ - mu*] *apsi šu - ut* ^{ilu}*E - a*

ḳaḳḳadu ḳarnu u šu - ku - su pa - nu ameli
[*li*]-*ta šakin(in) uzun alpi bur-ṣa-ṣa šaḳin(in)*
[*rit*]-*ta-šu ameli a-gu-uḫ-ḫa ina ir-ti-šu la-biš*
[*ḳatu*] - *šu ša imitti tar - ṣa - at - ma*
[GIŠ - BA - AN ?] - GAB - GAB - A *ga* . . . .
[*ina ḳati-šu*] *ša šumeli* ^{iṣu}*ḫu-up-pa-la-a* [*na-ši*]
. . . . *sip - pu - ra ra -* [*ki - is*]
. . . . *ḳa - tum su* . . . . . .
. . . .

COL. IV.

. . . . *ka pi* . . . . *ti*
[*rit-ti*]-*šu ameli ina imitti*-[*šu i*]-*ḳar-rab*
[*ina*] *šumeli - šu* ^{iṣu}*paššuri* (?) *na - ši*
[*kap*] - *pi šakin(in) sip - pu* - [*ra*] *ra - ki - is*

The base of his right foot is a bird's claw.
With the flat (?) of this sole also he touches (?).

(PLATE XLIV.)

The . . . is that of a lion, the body a naked *kissugu*,
His name is *Laḫmu ippiru*,
. . . *nutum* a monster of heaven and earth,
A sea-[monster], a form of Ea.

His head (has) a horn and . . . (?)[a] : the face of a man ;
He wears a headband ; the ear of an ox ; he wears a head-ornament ;
His fist is that of a man ; he is clothed with a doublet[b] on his breast.
His right [hand] is stretched out and
[holds ?] a bundle (?) ;
In his left [hand he holds] a . . . . . (?)
. . . . . he is girt about the loins ;
. . . .

COL. IV.

His [fist] is that of a man, inclining to the right,
In his left hand he holds a dish ;
He has wings ; he is girt about the loins ;

---

[a] *Šukusu* or *šutussu*, meaning unknown.

[b] *Aguḫḫu*, cf. Jensen, *Mythen und Epen*, p. 448.

---

iš - tu ti - ki - šu ana sip - pu - ra amelu
iš - tu sip - pu - ri - šu ana šepâ ^{II} *- [šu] kalbu*
. . *in - dur iṣṣuri šakin(in)* . . . *ka šakin(in)*
šum - šu Laḫ - mu šu - [ut] ^{ilu}*Gu - la*

ḳaḳḳadu ḳarnu u šu - ku - [su] pa - nu ameli
li - ta šakin(in) [bur - ṣa] - ṣa šakin(in)
ri - it - ta - šu ameli
ina imitti - šu ḫup - pa - [la - a ?] na - ši
ina šumeli - šu ^{iṣu}*mitpani u [izzi (?) na] - ši*
sip - pu - ra ra - ki - [is] . . . .
. . . *šu nûni ra - ki - [is]* . . . .
. . . .
. . . .
. . . . *ra* . . . .
. . . . *ḳaḳḳadu* . . . .
. . . . *sip - pu - ri - šu* . . . .

(PLATE XLV.)

[šum] - šu Šu - lu - ul . . . .

[ḳaḳḳa]du ku - ub - šu . . . .
uzun alpi šakin(in) šar - [tu iš - tu] . . . *u*
[ana ša] - šal - li - šu [na - da] - at
[pa] - nu . . . . *- tum*
[rit] - ta - šu ameli
[kap] - pi šakin - ma rit - ta - ša
. . . . . *ka kap - pi - ša tar - ṣa*
[pag] - ru me - ri - nu sinništum(tum) šepâ ^{II} *- šu*
ḫu - up - pa izzaza(za)
šum - šu Ni - zi - iḳ - tum

From the waist[a] to the loins he is a man,
From the loins to the feet he is a dog ;
He has the . . . (?) of a bird ; he has . . .
His name is Laḫmu, a form of Gula

The head (has) a horn and . . . . . (?) : the face of a man ;
He wears a headband ; he wears a head-ornament (?)
His fist is that of a man.
In his right hand he holds a . . . . . (?),
In his left hand he holds a bow and [arrows ?] ;
He is girt about the loins . . . .
His . . . is that of a fish, girt . . .
. . . .

(Plate XLV.)

His [name] is Šulul . . . . . .

The head (has) a fillet . . . .
He has the ear of an ox ; hair lies [from] . . .
As far as his shoulders (?)
The face is that of a . . . .
His fist is that of a man,
He has wings and the fist (?) . . .
. . . . . of the wing is spread out,
The body is a naked woman ; his legs stand bent (?)[b]
His name is Niziḳtum.

---

[a] *Tiki*, cf. the Hebrew *tawek*, cstr. *tok* (Gesenius, ed. Mühlan und Volck, 892, *b*).

[b] *Ḫuppa* = "broken." It is possible that this is in antithesis to "his left foot is stretched out" (l. 57).

[ḳaḳḳa]du ḳaḳḳad iṣṣuri ap - par - ra - tu
[ul] - tu ḳaḳḳadi - ša ana ša - šal - li - ša nadat
[rit] - ta - ša ameli
[ina ki - la] - te - ša GAR - NA *na - ša - at*
. . . *- šu imitti u šumeli šaknat(at) - ma*
[gil] - ta - nu šu - gal - lu - lu
[pag] - ru sinništum - (tum)
. . . . - *ḳa - tum* KAT - MAḪ
. . . . *- šu ša iṣṣuri*
*[šepâ*II *- ša] ḫu - up - pa izzaza(za)*
[šum - šu] ilu . . . .

K. 13,843.

a. *[ina] ki - la - te - šu* . . . . . *[na - ši]*
b. *šum - šu* ilu *Ti* . . . .

---

c. *ḳaḳḳadu ḳaḳḳad ki - is - su - [gi]*
d. *ina ri - it - ti - šu* . . . .
e. *[ina] imitti - šu i -* . . . .
. . . .

81–7–27, 109.

. . . .
g. . . *tu* . . . .
h. *šum - šu* . . . .

---

i. *ḳaḳḳadu ku - ub - šu* . . . .
j. *i - na eli* . . . .
k. ilu NIN - KIŠ - TIR - RA . . . .
l. *'pa - nu ameli* . . . .
m. *bur - ṣa - ṣa [šakin]*
n. *ri - it - ta - šu* . . . .
o. *ina ki - la - te - šu* . . . .
p. . . . . *[sip] - pu - ra* . . . .
. . . .

The head is the head of a bird ; a veil hangs from her head to her shoulders (?)
Her fist is that of a man,
In her two hands (?) she holds a torch,
She has a right and left . . . .
Beslavered with drops of water,
The body is that of a woman,
The . . . is that of a (?)
The . . . . is that of a bird,
Her legs stand bent (?)
[Her name] is the goddess . . . .

Legend of the Worm.

OBVERSE.

(PLATE L.)

. . . .

ul - tu ^{ilu}A - nu - um . . . .

šamu(u) ib - nu - u [ir - ṣi - tum]

ir - ṣi - tum ib - nu - u nârâti^{pl}

nârâti^{pl} ib - na - a a - tap - pa - ti

a - tap - pa - ti ib - na - a ru - šum - ta

ru - šum - ta ib - nu - u tu - ul - tu

il-lik tu-ul-tu ana pan ^{ilu}Šamši i-bak-ki

ana pan ^{ilu}E - a il - la - ka di - ma - a - ša

mi - na - a ta - at - ta - an - na a - na a - ka - li - ia

mi - na - a ta - at - ta - an - na a - na mun - zu - ḳi - ia

at - tan - nak - ki iṣ - ma ba - ši - il - ta

ar - ma - na - a ^{iṣu}uddi (?)

ana - ku am - mi - na an - na - a iṣ - ma ba - ši - il - ta

u ar - ma - na - a ^{iṣu}uddi (?)

šu - uḳ - ḳa - an - ni - ma ina bi - rit ši - in - ni

Tablet inscribed with the Legend of the Worm (B.M. No. 55,547).

(*To face p.* 160.)

Legend of the Worm.

OBVERSE.

(PLATE L.)

. . . .

After Anu [had created the Heavens],
The Heavens created [the Earth],
The Earth created the Rivers,
The Rivers created the Canals,
The Canals created the Marshes,
The Marshes created the Worm.
Came the Worm (and) wept before Shamash,
Before Ea came her tears :—
" What wilt thou give me for my food,
" What wilt thou give me for my devouring ? " [a]
" I will give thee dried bones,
" (And) scented . . . -wood."
" What are these dried bones to me,
" And scented . . . -wood ! "
" Let me drink among the teeth,

[a] *Munzuḳu* and *lunzuḳa* (l. 16), lit. " damage."

u la - aš - ḫi šu - ši - ba - an - ni
ša ši - in - ni - ma lu - un - zu - ḳa da - mi - šu

REVERSE.

u ša la - aš - ḫi - ši - im lu - uk - su - us
ku - sa - si - e - šu
sik - ka - ta dal - te - ma aṣ - ṣa - ba - at
aš - šum an - na - a taḳ - bi - i tu - ul - tu
lim - ḫa - aṣ - ki *ilu E - a i - na dan - na - ti*
ri - it - ti - šu

INIM - INIM - MA KA - GIG - GA - KAN

---

tippuš šuati šikari *sammu* SA-KIL-BIR *u šamni*
ištenis(nis) tuballal
šipti III-šu ana eli tamannu(nu) i-na eli ši-in-ni-šu
tašakkan(an)

GAB-RI IM-GID-DA *ša a-na pî ša-ṭar ṣar-pa la-bi-ri-im*
ša *m ilu Marduk-nadin-aḫi* *m ilu Nabu-na-din-ib-ri-a*
. . . . *nu* IN-SAR
. . . .

" And set me on the gums [a] ;
" That I may devour the blood of the teeth
" And of their gums destroy the strength ;
" Then shall I hold the bolt of the door."
So must thou say this : "O Worm !
" May Ea smite thee with the might of his fist."

Incantation of the Sick Mouth.

Thou shouldst do the following :
Mix beer, the plant SA-KIL-BIR, and oil together,
Repeat thereon the incantation thrice
(And) put it on his tooth.

[a] *Lašḫi*, meaning doubtful.

Vocabulary of Selected Words.

[NOTE.—Tablets 3, 4, 5, 10, 15, 16, and "A"–"K" are in Vol. I; Tablets "Aš. 3" (i.e. *Ašakku* III), "L," "M," "N," 11, 12, "Mu. 3" (i.e. *Muruṣ ḳaḳḳadi* or *Ṭi'i* III), 6, "O," 8, 9, "P"–"Z," "Lu. 8" (i.e. *Luḫ-ka* VIII), "AA"–"DD," and "Worm" (i.e. Legend of the Worm), are in Vol. II.]

i, "not": G, 7, 19, 13.

e, "not": 4, v, 62, [66, 68], vi, 2; 5, ii, 8; C, 67–91.

âru, "to start": I, 1, *'-ram-ma,* K, 77; *i-ir-ru,* 5, ii, 35; *'-ir-ru,* V, 24; *a-(a)-ri,* K, 69; *a-ri,* V, 47; II, 1, *li-ru-šu,* V, 47; I, 2 (?), *i-ta-ru-uš,* 5, vi, 2.

abbu, "serpent (?)": cf. Arabic حُبَاب, 16, 22.

ibiḫu, ?: P, 24.

abru, "nest": 4, i, 35.

ubbutu, see *upputu.*

agubbu, "water, laver": 3, 256; 16, 208; N, iii, 3; AA, 52, 68, 70, 74, 75, 76, 77.

aguḫḫu, "doublet": DD, 77.

igîru (?): III, 2, *šu-te-gu-rat,* DD, 67.

egirtum, egirru, "thought": 3, 281.

iddû, "bitumen": 16, 305.

ittu, "appearance": M, 27.

idîdu, "be straight": I, 1, *id-da-at,* DD, 28.

edêlu, "to shut": I, 1, *li-di-lu,* V, 75.

izîru, "to trickle": II, 1, *uz-zu-ru,* DD, 16.

aḫḫazu, "a demon, robber sprite": 3, 196; 4, v, 20; 5, i, 50; C, 83, 98; D, iii, 37; K, 261; V, 18.

uḫulu, "alkali": AA, 38.

A-ḪA-AN-TUM, ? 3, 199.

[IḪ-TAG]-GA-A-MU-NE, "in my soreness": 4, v, 50.

IḪ-TUK-A-MU-NE, variant of above: 5, ii, 1.

eṭû, "to be dark": II, 1, *uṭ-ṭu-u*, K, 35; II, 2, *u-ta-aṭ-ṭu-u*, C, 140.

eṭutu, "gloom": 16, 37.

makalû, "food": Á, iv, 18.

ikîlu, "to be dark": IV, 3, *i-te-ni-ik-ki-la*, V, 81.

ikîmu, "to rob": I, 1, *e-kim*, B, 21; X, 2.

ekimmu, "ghost": 3, 12, 33, 100, 112, 154, 162, 195; 4, iv, 43, v, 6, 8, 10, 12, 14; 5, iii, 27, 45, iv, 15, 16; 10, 10; 16, 211, 262, 283, 309; A, i, 5, 35, 45, ii, 30, iii, 31, iv, 18, 20; C, 71, 97, 122, 157, 174; D, iii, 36, 38; E, 52; G, 4; K, 217, 260; Aš. 3, 26; L, 6; N, iv, 6, vii, 8; 8, 31; 11, 10, 91, 97; T, 6, r. 23; V, 16; CC, 2.

akâšu, "to go furtively," a synonym of *alâku*, *Cun. Texts*, pt. xviii, pl. 6, obv. 53, followed by *dâlu*: I, 1, *i-ku-uš*, T, 6; [. . -*ku* ?]-*uš-ma*, 9, 135.

alû, "devil": 3, 12, 31, 100, 112, 154, 162, 195; 5, iii, 27, 45; 10, 8; 16, 210, 262, 281, 309; A, 9, 34, 43, ii, 29, iii, 29; B, 3 ff., 55, 79, 81, 95; C, 60, 97, 188; D, iii, 36; E, 52; G, 4; K, 13, 217, 260; L, 4; N, iii, 26, iv, 4, 6, 16; 8, 27, 31; 11, 91, 97; 12, 38, [65]; 9, 8, 238; P, 10; T, 16; U, 1; V, 16; CC, 2.

elû, "to go up": I, 2, *li-til-la*, 9, 89.

alluḫappu, "sack": B, 41.

alâku, "to go": III, 1, *u-ša-lik*, N, ii, 22.

alallu, "bundle": P, 64; cf. AA, 63, and DD, 79.

ulinnu, "cord," probably Syriac ܗܠܢܐ: 16, 181; D, iii, 17.

alapu, ?: I, 1, *al-pu*, X, 11.

iltu, "straw": 9, 50.

emêdu, "to stand": II, 1, *um-mu-di-ia*, 3, 152; IV, 1, [*in*]-*nim-mi-du*, E, 28.

umunnû, "disease": 3, 45.

ininnu, kind of corn: 9, 129.

unḳâti, "rings": DD, 19.

usuzzu, "standing": CC, 8.

asammû, kind of vessel : A, 19.
aspasti (?), *Medicago sativa* : B, 27 (?).
asurrû, "chamber" : C, 216.
upû, "cloud" : 9, 24.
uppu, "cloudy": 5, ii, 66 (read thus instead of *ubbutum*); P, 11, 27.
apparu, "cane-brake": 16, 296*a*.
apparratu, "headband," Hebrew אֲפֵר : DD, 113.
apparritu, variant of above : DD, 4, 20.
upišu, "enchantment" : 3, 58 ; C, 182 ; E, 9.
iḳbu, "heel," Hebrew עָקֵב : DD, 23.
iṣmu, "bone," Heb. עֶצֶם (cf. *iṣṣimtu*, King, *The Seven Tablets of Creation*, vol. i, p. 86) : Worm, 11, 13.
eṣênu, "to stink" : II, 1, *uṣ-ṣa-nu*, C, 216.
aru, "date-spathe" : 3, 213.
irru, ? : P, 35.
eru, "tamarisk," Syriac ܥܪܳܐ : 3, 87, 211 ; 16, 249 ; K, 140.
eru, "meteorite" : 16, 247 ; A, 27, 32 ; N, ii, 11.
erêbu, "to enter" : I, 2, *mu-tir-ru*-(v. *ri*)-*bu*, C, 104.
urbatu, perhaps to be connected with the Syriac ܐܪܒܢܐ, "a reed," but more probably with ܥܪܒܬܐ, "a willow" : 9, 71 ; P, 36.
ardatu, "maiden, woman" : 3, 197 ; 4, i, 27, iv, 45 ; C, 89, 99 ; 9, 152 ; T, 10 ; V, 20 ; Lu. 8, 14 ; AA, 16.
arḫu, "cow": S, 3, 30 ; AA, 46.
armanû, "scent" : Worm, 12, 14.
urinnu, "cloud" : K, 35 ; DD, 24 (?).
erinu, "cedar" : 12, 58 ; 9, 229 ; AA, 43.
arsuppu, "parsnip (?)," Syriac ܦܘܪܣܦܐ (?) : 9, 129.
uriṣu, "kid" : E, 38 ; F, iii, 2, iv, 3, 6, 8 ; 11, 24, 74, 84 ; N, iii, 46, 48, 50, 52, 54 ; 8, ii, 26.
arâṣu, "to meet, march," Syriac ܐܪܰܥ : I, 1, *ia-ru-uṣ*, 3, 265.
arâru, "to tremble" : I, 1, *tar-ru*, G, 9 ; IV, 3, *it-ta-na-ar-ra-ru*, 16, 103 ; *it-ta-nu-ur-ru*, V, 42.
urtu, "explanation," K, 111.
ešû, "to set" : I, 1, *e-ša-a*, 16, 336.

ešitum, 15, 13.

ašâbu, "to sit": II, 1, *u-šub-šum-ma*, A, 30.

ašakku, "fever": 3, 4., 117, 156, 164. 179, 198; 5, ii, 4, 6, 8, 10, iii, 40; A, ii, 15; C, 96, 100; I, 1, 2; J, 5; L, 16; M, 1; 11, 2, 46, 93, 102, 105; 12, 2; O, 6, 12; 9, 3; R, 4; S, 4; V, 22; BB, 1.

ušultu, "vein": 5, iv, 27.

ušumgallum, "dragon": 16, 15.

ašamšutum, "tempest": 16, 32.

išipputu, "priestcraft": AA, 60

eššepu, "owl," Heb. יַנְשׁוּף (Delitzsch): 5, i, 21.

ašašu, "to oppress": I, 1, *i-aš-ša-šu*, 5, iii, 42; *i-aš-ša-a-su*, 10, 8; *taš-ša-aš-šu*, A, 47; II, 2, *u-ta-aš-ši-iš*, 11, 71.

atû, "to see": I, 1, *a-ta-*[*a*], 3, 261; *a-ta-at*, DD, 12; II, 1, *ut-tu-šu*, S, r. 11.

ututu, "chosen": DD, 41.

ittu, ?: B, 75.

ittû, "pitch": P, 26.

utukku, "spirit": 3, 29, 100, 112, 153, 154, 162, 194, 195; 4, i, 41, v, 29, vi, 45; 5, i, 4, 35, iii, 27, 45. vi, 2, 21, 24; 10, 6; 16, 110, 262, 281, 308, 309; A, 34, 43, ii, 29, iii, 18, 21, 27, 43, 44, 46; B, 79, 93; C, *c*, *e*, 41, 58, 67, 97, 118, 157, 168, 174, 180, 187, 195; D, iii, 38; E, 15, 52; H, r. 7; J, 9; K, 221, 260, 265; Aš. 3, 28; L, 3, 8, 15; N, ii, 11, iii, 26, 27, iv, 2, vii, 13; 11, 91; W, 3; and *passim* in INIM-INIM-MA UTUG-ḪUL-A-KAN.

ŭtlu, "embrace": 4, ii, 25, v, 52; 5, i, 37, ii, 41; R, 34.

atappatu, "canal": Worm, 4, 5.

atru, "abundant, fat (?)": 11, 26.

bâ'u, "to come": I, 1, *i-ba-'-u*, 16, 145; III, 1, *šu-bi-'-šu-ma*, N, iii, 6; *šu-bi-i-'-ma*, T, r. 4; *šu-bi-'* . . . ; AA, 79, 81–83, 85; U-ME-NI-E, A, i, 22; 11, 86; T, r. 6.

buanu, "muscle": 3, 182; 11, 52; 9, 8; P, 17, 23; AA, 37.

ba'âru, "to hunt": I, 3, *ib-ta-na-'-rum*, X, 10.

babâlu, "to bring": IV, 1, *ib-bab-la*, E, 40; AA, 44.

buḫattu, "lamb": 16, 182.

baltu, "caper (?)," Syriac ܒܠܛ: B, 75.

banû, "be bright": II, 1, [*bu-u*]*n-nu-u*, D, iv, 42.

bennu, "pestilence": N, 7.

burṣaṣu, Chaldee בֻּרְצִין: DD, 3, 76; 81-7-27, 109, *m*.

barâru, "to howl": IV, 2, *it-ta-ab-ra-ru*, K, 31.

burašu, "cypress": AA, 40.

bašiltu, "dried": Worm, 11, 13.

GI-BIL-LA, "torch": A, i, 22, ii, 23; K, 279; N, iii, 5; 11, 86; T, r. 6.

gallû, "devil": 3, 100, 112, 154, 162, 195; 5, iii, 27, 45, iv, 15, 17, 33; 10, 12; 16, 263, 283, 310; A, 35, 45, ii, 30, iii, 33; C, 73, 97, 122; D, iii, 36; E, 52; G, 4; K, 217, 260; L, 7; N, iv, 8, vii, 22; Mu. 3, 33; 8, 32, ii, 10, 11, 12; T, r. 8, 24; V, 16; X, 5, 6, 7; CC, 2.

galâlu, "to be beslavered": III, 1; *šu-gal-lu-lu*, DD, 18; *šu-gal-lu-lu-ni*, DD, 17.

galâtu, "to frighten": II, 1; *gul-lu-ti-ia*, 3, 188; III, 1, *šug-lit-ma*, 9, 128.

galtu, "terrible": 16, 20, 248; A, 26.

gallutu, "quaking": N, 15.

giltanu, "drop of water": DD, 118.

GI-SAG-DA-DI-*u*, "reed hat (?)": 8, 29.

GI-SAG-DU-DI-A, "reed hat (?)": 8, 22.

gipâru, "field": 5, vi, 14.

GAR-NA, "censer": A, i, 22, ii, 23; 11, 86; N, iii, 5; T, r. 6; DD, 116.

gurgurru, "coppersmith": F, iii, 11.

U-*GURU-UŠ-RIG-AN-BAR-KA-A-NI (?): 9, 201.

gišparru, "snare": V, 12, 26.

dâlu, "to move furtively," cf. Syr. ܕܳܠ: I, 1, *i-dul* (v. *i-dul-lu*, v. *i-du-*[*ul*]), B, 45; *i-da-al*, T, 8; II, 1, *mu-dal-la*, B, 67.

da(d)danu: see Mu. 3, 1; 9, 101.

dinanu, "substitute": 8, 29; W, 2; see Vol. II, p. 2, note *b*.

dapâru, "to remove"; II, 1, *dup-pir*, 3, 158; 10, r. 2; E, 50; ? 3, 202; II, 1, (?) *ud-da-pa-ru*, N, ii, 36.

dušû, a stone: AA, 50.

dišpu, "honey": Aš. 12, 57.

zu'unu, "battening," Heb. זון: 5, v, 33.
zamanu, "enemy (?)": 12, 6.
zarâbu, "to restrain": II, 1, *u-zar-ri-*[*ib* ?], B, 77.
zaraḳu, "to sprinkle": *zi-ri-i*[*ḳ-mà*], 3, 8.
ḫîlu, "to tremble": I, 1, *ta-ḫal*, G, 7.
ḫâpu, "to wash" Syr. ܚܦ: I, 1 (?), IM-*DAR-RA, D, 23.
naḫbalu, "snare": P, 15.
haṣbu, "pot": C, 171.
ḫulû, "fleabane (?)," Syr. ܚܠܐ: B, 73.
ḫulduppû: see note, Vol. I, p. 160; D, iii, 32, 34; F, iii, 13; K, 140; 11, 104; 12, 61.
ḫalâlu, "to creep": IV, 3, *it-ta-na-aḫ-lal-lu*, K, 103.
ḫulalu, a stone: AA, 50.
halâṣu, "to tear": IV, 1, *iḫ-ḫi-il-ṣa-a*, 4, v, 2.
sammu ḪUL-TI-GIL-LA, "wild cucumber (?)": 9, 37.
ḫamû, "to scorch," Syr. ܚܡܐ: I, 1, *iḫ-mu-šu*, A, 11; *iḫ-me-šu*, 9, 14.
ḫamâṭu, "to burn": I, 1, *i-ḫa-am-ma-ṭu*, K, 288; II, 1, *u-ḫa-am-maṭ*, P, 18; *mu-ha-am-me-ṭu*, P, 17; *ḫum-mu-du*, 11, 18; II, 2, *uḫ-tam-maṭ*, 9, 22.
ḫamru, ?: 9, 24.
ḫinnu, "henna," Arabic حِنَّاء: *kanu* *ḫi-ni*, 9, 8; *kanu* *ḫi-in-nu*, P, 31.
ḫinzu, "mucus (?)": DD, 16.
iṣu **ḫuppalû,** (?): DD, 80, 94.
ḫupdi . . . , (?): DD, 26.
ḫuppu, "bent (?)": DD, 119, 122.
haṣbu, "potsherd, pot": P, 13; V, 63.
haṣâsu, "to slit": II, 2, *uḫ-ta-aṣ-ṣi-iṣ* (v. *ṣi*), 9, 6.
ḫarû, "ditch": P, 45.
ḫarbu, "desolate": B, 99.
ḫarbašu, "rain," "terror (?)": 3, 199; 4, vi, 44; 5, i, 3.
sammu ḪAR-ḪAR, a plant: 9, 200.
ḫarasu, "to split": I, 2, *iḫ-ta-ra-as*, R, 14.
hašu, "to hasten": I, 1, *ḫi-šam-ma*, K, 124.
ḫittu, "lintel": B, 73.

ṭi'u, "headache": 3, 199; A, i, 9, iii, 36; O, 4, 12; 9, 28, 101, 148, 193; P, 2, 22, 52, 77; BB, 3.

ṭiṭu, "clay": K, 30, 42.

ṭimû, "weave": I, 1, *ṭi-me*, 16, 182; [6, 6]; [*ṭi*]-*me*, 9, 231.

ṭappu, "sole, palm," Heb. טֶפָח: DD, 11, 32, 36, 38, 58, 68, 70.

kipû, "to bend": I, 1, *kap-pat*, DD, 31.

kûru, "pain": 5, i, 43.

kîru, "pitch (?)": N, ii, 5.

kubšu, "fillet": DD, 2, 26, 42, 104; 81–7–27, 109, *i*.

kabati, "heavy (?)": U, 3.

kudurru: AA, 40.

kakkultu, "bason": V, 79.

kilate, "both (hands) (?)": DD, 30, 53, 116: K. 13,843*a*; 81–7–27, 109, *o*.

kilalli, "both": P, 66; AA, 34.

kilallan, "both": K, 198.

kalâpu, "to move": IV, 1, *muk-kal-pi-te*, O, 4; 9, 55.

kuliptu, "scales," Syr. ܡܠܦܬܐ: DD, 12, 39.

kultu, "canopy," Chald. כִּילְתָא: K, 117.

kamanu, "cake": Aš. 3, 13.

kamâru, "to fall": I, 2, *kit-mu-ru*, P, 79.

kanakku, some part of a door: V, 59.

kanu, "base," Heb. כֵּן: DD, 11, 23, 32, 35, 36.

kanû, "to guard": II, 1, *u-kan-ni*, P, 43; *u-kan-na*, P, 43.

kinzu, "flat of the footsole (?)": DD, 58.

kissugu, (?): DD, 49, 71; K, 13,843*c*.

kiskibirru (?): A, ii, 28.

kasâsu, "to destroy": I, 1, *lu-uk-su-us*, Worm, 18.

kusasû, "destruction": Worm, 19.

kasâpu, "to pay rites": I, 1, *ka-sa-ap*, Y, 9.

kusurru, "bandage (?)": A, ii, 25; D, iii, 22, 23; 11, 89; V, 28.

kiṣu in **kiṣ libbi,** "heartache (?)": A, 9, 37; C, 95; D, iii, 41; 11, 100; 9, 18, 116; BB, 3.

kippatu, "twig," Heb. כִּפָּה: P, 64; AA, 63.

kippatu, "end, corner": Mu. 3, 6.

kapâdu, "to found": I, 1, *i-kap-pu-ud*, 16, 80.
kapâru, "to atone": II, 1, *kup-pir*, 11, 85; R, 36; T, 40; *ku-up-pir*, 8, 24; *u-kap-pi-ru*, U, 18.
takpirtu, "atonement": Aš. 3, 5.
kiṣṣuru, "girt about": A, 49.
karû, "to bend": I, 1, *ki-ra-at*, DD, 27.
sammu KUR-KUR, a plant: 9, 200.
kurpu, "dungheap (?)": Aš. 3, 7.
karâṣu, "to pull off": I, 1, *ki-ri-iṣ-ma*, R, 31.
karru, "destruction": 5, i, 11.
karâru, "to turn": I, 1, *ka-ra-ri-e*, K, 150; IV, 3, *it-ta-nak-ra-ru*, 9, 18.
karašu, "leek": R, 14; S, 14; T, 12.
kiškanû, Astragalus, Tragacanth (?): K, 184, 201.
katimtu, "coverlet": B, 39.
li'u, ?: 11, 85; 9, 134; T, 38.
la-a-tu, "cow": Mu. 3, 30.
lu-'-a-ti, "unclean": B, 23.
litu, "strength": 3, 190.
lîtu, "headband," Heb. לִוְיָה: DD, 20, 45, 92.
liaru, a tree: AA, 40.
lublubu, "trap (?)": P, 15.
labnu: see 11, 50.
labaṣu, "ghoul": 3, 35, 196; 4, v, 18; 5, i, 49, iii, 24; A, i, 7, 36; C, 81, 98; D, iii, 37; K, 261; 11, 92, 98; V, 18.
labartu, "hag-demon": 3, 35, 196; 4, v, 16; 5, i, 48, iii, 22, 24; A, i, 36; C, 79, 98; D, iii, 37; K, 261, 282; 11, 92, 98; 8, 33; P, 5; V, 18.
labuttu, "chief": 4, iv, 3.
laḫmu, "monster": DD, 25, 61, 73, 74, 90.
laḫru, "shoots (?)": 5, iv, 31.
lilû, "phantom": 3, 37, 156, 164, 197; C, 85, 89, 99; K, 262; V, 20.
lilitu, feminine of above: 3, 156, 164, 197; C, 87, 99; K, 262; V, 20.
lamâdu, "to learn": I, 1, *la-mit-tu*, 4, iv, 45.

lamassu, "guardian spirit": 3, 9, 94, 153, 194, 287; 16, 289, 308, 346; K, 206, 225; L, 9; Aš. 12, 66; 6, 14; 8, 28, vi, 17, 35, 36; 9, 7, 239.

lamṣati, "fly (?)": DD, 3.

lânu, "shape": P, 10.

lipitum (?): 4, iv, 35.

lašḫu, "gum of the teeth (?)": Worm, 17, 18.

miṭru, "rain (?)," Heb. מָטָר: 12, 24.

milu, "full strength (?)": R, 18; S, 18.

sammu MULU-GIŠGAL-LU, a plant: 9, 200.

malâlu, "to cry," Syr. ܡܠܠ: IV, 1, *im-ma* (v. *me*)-*lil-lu*, K, 101.

mamitu, "ban, *tapu*": 3, 43; 5, ii, 2, 6, iv, 37; A, ii, 32; C, 182; D, iii, 28.

massû, "guide": 16, 58, 125.

maṣu, "be broad": II, 1, *mu-uṣ-ṣi-ma*, N, ii, 54.

merin(n)u, "naked (?)": DD, 59, 71, 111, *sal merinu*, DD, 10.

marâsu, "to mash up": I, 1, *mu-ru-us*, Aš. 3, 13, 14.

mirsu, "a mash": Aš. 3, 13, 14.

maruštu, "pain": 3, 117; 16, 7, 344; T, r. 13; U, 25.

mašû, "to rob": I, 1, *im-šu-'-u*, K, 53; II, 1, *muš-šu-u*, Mu. 3, r. 26.

mašu, "to forget": III, 2, *uš-tam-šu-u*, Mu. 8, 17.

maššiu, "robber": 5, iii, 17; 9, 185.

mušgarru, a stone: AA, 50.

mašâdu, "to bring low": I, 1, *ma-ša-di-ia*, 3, 190.

mašḫati (?), "libations of oil (?)," Syr. ܡܫܚܐ: K, 47.

mašlu, "middle": K, 154; Aš. 3, 12.

mašâtu, "to humble": I, 1, *im-ši-it*, 11, 48.

maštakal, a plant: A, i, 20; T, 31; AA, 37.

ni'u, "to turn": I, 1, *ni-'-i*, B, 55; G, 13.

ni'u, "restraint (?)": 16, 22.

nâru, "to smite": I, 1, *i-nar-ru*, 3, 29; 4, i, 43; *na-a-ri*, 16, 11.

nirtu, "destruction": 16, 11, 47.

nâšu, "to quake": II, 1, *u-na-aš* (v. *-a-šu*), P, 20: *nu-uš šu* (v. *ši*), 9, 53.

nigiṣṣu, "cavern": B, 35; K, 89, 103.

nagiru, "patron": 3, 90; 5, v, 22; K, 288.

nidutu, "desolate place": K, 91, 105; N, iii, 18.

nadâru, "to rage": I, 1, *na-ad-ru*, 5, iv, 25; *na-ad-ru* (v. *ri*), 16, 22.

mazaltu, "homestead": 9, 89.

nazâḳu, "to destroy": I, 1, *lu-un-zu-ka*, Worm, 17.

munzuḳu, "destruction": Worm, 10.

niziḳtum, name of a demon or god: DD, 112.

naṭû, "to be fit": *na-ṭu-u*, 9, 53.

niṭlu, "brightness": B, 43.

nikibtu, ?: AA, 43.

nakâlu, "to be cunning": I, 1, *nak-lat* (v. *la-at*), B, 53; *nik-la-ma*, 4, vi, 2; BA-GUB-BA, 5, ii, 62.

nukušû, part of a door: V, 59.

nalâšu, "to rain": I, 1, *ina-al-lu-uš*, Aš. 12, 4.

nalšu, "rain": Aš. 12, 4.

namû, "ruins": B, 57, 95.

namâšu, "to circle": I, 1, *ta-nam-miš* (v. *mi*-[*iš*]), A, iv, 28.

namtaru, "pestilence": 3, 46, 117, 156, 164, 179; 5, i, 7, ii, 50, iii, 8, 40; A, 24, iii, 35, 42; C, 100, 158, 176; J, 7; 11, 4, 93, 102; R, 40; T, r. 8; V, 22; W, 4.

nasâku, "to put, place": I, 1, *u-suk-ma*, 9, 38; I, 2, *i-ta-as-suk-ma*, N, iii, 9.

napâṣu, "to lay low": I, 1, *i-nap-pa-ṣu*, T, 10.

niḳû, "to slay": I, 1, *ni-ḳa-a*, B, 27; *i-naḳ-ḳi*, K, 49; I, 1, *it-ta-ḳi*, 12, 44.

naḳû, "libation": 4, v, 12; Y, 9.

naḳâru, "to destroy": I, 1, *i-na-ḳar*.

narâbu, "to break": IV, 1, *mun-nar-bi*, B, 77.

naruḳku, "girdle": cf. Syr. ܢܪܘܬܐ; A, iv, 12.

narârû, "to help": I, 1, *na-ri-ru*, B, 65.

našâku, "to bite": I, 1, *iš-šuk* (v. *šu-uk*), 16, 131.

našâru, "to bring low": I, 1, *i-na-aš-ša-ru*, T, r. 13; II, 1, *mu-na-aš-šir*, 5, i, 3, iv, 9, 11; BA-NIGIN-NA-BA-E, 4, vi, 44.

natânu, rare bye-form of *nadânu*, "to give": I, 1, *at-tan-nak-ki*, Worm, 11; *ta-at-ta-an-na*, Worm, 9, 10.

sâbu, "to bale up (?)": I, 1, *sa-am-ma*, AA, 34.
sâmu, "brown (?)": B, 69, 71; AA, 50.
suntu, "side, loins": K, 57.
sâpu, "to perish," Syr. ܣܳܦ: II, 1, *u-sip-pu*, K, 63.
sibû, "seven": 16, 26.
sibburu, DD, 5, 9, 11, 54, 65, 81, 86, 87, 88, 96, 102; 81–7–27, 109, *p*.
SAG-KI, "temples (?)": 9, 192, 209, 210.
suddinnu, "bat (?)": B, 35.
SUḪ-ḪA, a fish: DD, 21.
suḫuššu, ?: T, 31; AA, 37.
saḫâpu, "to spread over": I, 1, *i-sa-ḫap*, 12, 40; *i-saḫ-ḫa-pu*, B, 41; *saḫ-pu*, K, 41.
saḫputum, "widespreading": K, 35.
SAḪ-TUR-RA, "little pig": 3, 40; L, 14; N, ii, 44, 53, iii, 10, 11, 28.
sammu SA-KIL-BIR, a plant: Worm, 25.
sakâru, "to clog": I, 1, *i-sik* (v. *sak*)-*kir*, P, 26; *i-sak-kir*, P, 47.
sikkuru, "bolt": V, 53, 55.
samanu, "poison (?)": C, 96.
sanâḳu, "to reach": I, 1, *sa-niḳ* . . . F, iv, 21; *is-niḳ*, K, 121; *tasaniḳ*, 5, v, 24.
Sassu-urinnu, name of a monster: DD, 24.
sisit, "fingers (?)": DD, 51.
sapû, "to gather together," Syr. ܣܦܳܐ: I, 1, *i-sa-ap-pu-'*, A, 14.
supalu, ?: AA, 40.
sapânu, "to cover": I, i, *i-sap-pa-nu*, K, 29.
saparu, "net"; K, 148; O, 12; V, 14, 30; BB, 10.
saru, "to putrefy," Syr. ܣܪܝ: I, 1, *i-sa-ri*, Mu. 3, 2.
sarâḳu, "to pour": I, 2, *is-sar-rak*, K, 47.
pûdu, "flanks": P, 30.
pûḫu, "stead, substitute": Aš. 3, 7; N, iii, 11 [23].
pîru, "young, offspring": 16, 18.
pâšu, "axe": F, iii, 14.
puzru, "secret": G, 7; K, 41.

puzurtu, "secret": K, 121.
paḫaru, "potter": C, 171.
pikurtu, "cord": 6, 6; 9, 231.
palâku, "to cut off": I, 1, *i-pal-lik*, P, 37.
palâlu, "to scatter," Syr. ܦܠ: I, 1, *i-pa-al-li-lu*, C, 126.
papanu, "navel" (?): DD, 13.
piṣû, "white": 11, 74; S, r. 5.
paḳu (?), ?: 16, 232.
puḳlu, "tow," Chald. פּוּקְלָא: P, 27.
parâ'u, "to cut off": I, 1, *pu-ru-'-ma*, P, 74; *i-par-ra-'*, P, 29.
piri'u, cf. Syr. ܦܪܥܐ, hypericum: B, 75.
puridu, "therefore": 16, 123; R, 24.
parittum, cf. Syr. ܦܪ, fugit: P, 5.
parâku, "to block up": I, 1, *pi-rik-[ma]*, Aš. 3, 10.
parâku, "to have power over": I, 1, *par-ku*, A, 43, 45; *ip-rik*, T, 4.
purimu, "wild ass": 9, 24.
pursitu, "separated": C, 171.
parištu, "wise woman": 9, 76.
puršumtu, "old woman": K, 271 (?); 9, 133.
pušḳu, "misery": N, ii, 41.
paštu, "flax," Heb. פִּשְׁתָּה: 16, 299; U, 33.
pitiktu, "mud-wall": C, 186.
patinnu, "girdle": 11, 52.
ṣa'âdu, "to hunt": I, 1, *ṣa-i-du*, 4, i, 41; *ṣa-i-du-ti*, 4, i, 41; IV, 3, *iṣ-ṣa-nun-du*, 5, iii, 12; 16, 32; C, 16, 22, 124; X, 9, 12.
ṣa'ânu, "to fill": I, 1, *ṣi-in-šu-ma*, 11, 38; I, 2, (?) *iṣ-ṣa-nu-uš*, A, 11; *iṣ-ṣa-an*, K, 278, 280, 282, 284, [286]; II, 1, *u-ṣa-in-šu*, N, ii, 20.
ṣâru, "to weaken": I, 1, *i-ṣa-ar*, P, 23, 24; *ṣa-'-i-rat*, 16, 340.
ṣabâru, "to chirp," Syr. ܨܦܪ: I, 1, *i-ṣab bu-ru*, 5, i, 15; II, 2, *mu-uṣ-ṣab ra-tum*, T, r. 20.
ṣilu, "side": P, 33; V, 70.
ṣariru, a metal: AA, 50.
sirru, "hinge," Syr. ܨܝܪܐ: 4, ii, 23; 5, i, 35; 16, 258; V, 57.

ḳu, "cord": 16, 178, 336; 9, 185; P, 29.
ḳulu, "snare," Chald. קוֹלָא: 4, ii, 19.
ḳûlu, "burning": 5, i, 43; 9, 128.
ḳâpu, "to fall": I, 1, *i-ḳup-pu*, B, 5; *ḳa-bi* (?), 15, r. 6.
ḳabru, "grave": 4, i, 10; E, 23; Y, 3, 6, 10; Sm. 291, i, 11.
ḳadištu, "prostitute": 4, iv, 33; 5, i, 51.
ḳaṭnu, "little"; P, 35.
ḳimû, "flour": 5, iv, 21; Aš. 3, 10; 9, 37.
ḳumaru, "armlet," Syr. ܩܡܙܢܐ: DD, 50.
ḳinnu, "nest": 4, i, 37.
ḳinazu, "halter": B, 77.
ḳarnanu, "horned": A, 38.
ḳakû, ?: AA, 83.
ḳatû, "to end": II, 2, *uḳ-ta-at-ti*, 9, 150.
ḳutrinnu, "smoke-offering": D, iii, 19; E, 40.
rîtu, "pasture": 5, i, 45.
rûṣu, "to help": I, 1, *lu-ri-ṣu-ka*, A, 30; ḪU-MU-RA-AB-TAḪ-E, A, 32.
rîḳu, "to be distant": I, 1, *ir-te-iḳ*, R, 28; II, 1, *u-ri-iḳ*, U, 6, 7, 8.
rabiṣu, a demon: 3, 24 100, 112, 114, 154, 162, 195; 5, iii, 27, 45; 16, 211, [263]; A, i, 35; C, 77, 97, 120; D, iii, 36; G, 4; K, 217, 260; N, 11; 8, 33, ii, 30; V, 16.
ridû, "to seize, hold": I, 1, *ar*(v. *ir*)-*di-šu*, B, 67; *te-rid-di-šu*, 4, iv, 15; I, 2, *ir-te-di*, 5, vi, 4, 6; *mur-te-id-du-u*, 5, iv, 41.
ruḫû, "witchcraft": 3, 53*a*; C, 107*a*; K, 263; Lu. 8, 15; AA, 17.
riḫû, "to spawn": I, 1, *ri-ḫu-u*, 3, 240; 5, i, 4, 23; *i-ri-iḫ-ḫu-u*, B, 19; X, 7; A-RI-A-MEŠ, 3, 299; A-RI-A, 4, vi, 45.
riḫutu, "spawning": 4, i, 2, vi, 45; 5, i, 4, 23, iv, 41, v, 2.
riḫitu, "dregs": 9, 91.
ruk . . .: D, iii, 8.
ramâmu, "to shriek": I, 1, *i-ra-mu-um*, 9, 107.
rusû, "sorcery": 3, 53*a*; C, 107*a* (?); K, 263.
russu, ?: 3, 69, 107*h*.
riṣatum, ?: 9, 169.
riḳu, ?: AA, 40.

rušumtu, "marsh": T, 22; Worm, 5, 6.

ruššu, "skin (?)": 9, 183.

ruštu, "balsam (?)," Chald. רִיחוּשׁ: 12, 58; AA, 43.

ritû, "to set": I, 1, *ri-tu-u*, V, 12.

rittu, "fist, hand": DD, 4, 29, 51, 52, 77, 93, 108, 109, 115; K. 13,843*d*; 81–7–27, 109*n*; Worm, 23.

šêdu, "genius": 3, 92, 153, 285; 5, iv, 9, 11; 16, 4, 346*a*; G, 15; K, 206, 223, 282; L, 5, 10; N, 11, ii, 36, iii, 27; 6, 16; 11, 96; T, 4.

šîḫu, "lofty": P, 36.

šûlu, "cough," Syr. ܫܘܥܠܐ: Mu. 3, r. 20.

šârtu, "hair": 16, 171, 182, 316; 9, 43, 74; S, r. 5; DD, 33, 43, 105.

šertu, "wickedness": 3, 50, 50*a*.

šutu, "form": DD, 14, 25, 61, 74, 90.

šibbu, "serpent": 16, 20.

šabâṭu, "to smite": I, 1, *i-šab-bi-ṭu*, 4, i, 39; T, 9.

šabâru, "to break": III, 1, *u-ša-aš-*[*bir?*], P, 22.

šibru, "wood (?)": U, 10.

šagâmu, "to howl": I, 1, *i-šag-gu-mu*, 5, i, 15, 21; [*ta-šag-gum?*], C, 52.

šagâšu, "to rend in pieces": I, 1, *i-šag-gi-šu*, C, 134; *ša-ga-aš*, T, 8; *ša-ga-ša*, T, 6.

šigušu, a wood: 9, 129.

šaḫâḫu, "to waste": II, 1, *u-šaḫ-ḫa-aḫ*, 9, 10; P, 20.

šaḫâlu, "to draw forth," Chald. שְׁחַל: I, 1, *i-šaḫ-ḫa-lu*, C, 136; *i-šaḫ-ḫa-lum*, X, 15.

šaḫarru, "pot": 3, 56.

šaḫarratu, "vessel": P, 22; AA, 31.

šikku, "mouse": C, 216.

GIŠ-ŠA-KA-NA, "door": 16, 305; 8, ii, 17.

šil(l)ibu, "fox": B, 45.

šalâṭu, "to slit": I, 1, *i-šal-laṭ*, P, 31; II, 1, *u-šal-liṭ*, 9, 8.

šalalu, Syr. ܫܠ (?): *radix nymphœæ loti*, T, 31; AA, 37.

šulul, . . . name of a monster: DD, 103.

šalâpu, "to break out": I, 1, *šal-pat*, 9, 122.
šalâšu, "to triple": III, 1, *šu-uš-[lu-uš]*, 6, 6: *šu-uš-lu-[uš]*, 9, 231.
ša[maḫ]ḫu, "stout-hearted (?)": P, 35.
sammu ŠI-MAN, a plant: 9, 199.
šalû(?), "to sink": II, 1 (?), NAM-BA-IM-[IM-E-NE], 16, 258.
šapitum, "dense": 16, 34.
šapâku, "to pour out": I, 1, *šu-pu-uk*, A, 19; *šu-puk*, AA, 66.
šapâṣu (?), "to touch (?)": I, 1, *ša-pi-iṣ*, DD, 65, 66, 68, 70.
šapparu, "wild goat": S, 3, 8; P, 43.
šarbâṭu, "to roam": IV, 3, *it-ta-[na-aš-rab-bi-ṭu ?]*, C, 44; *it-ta-na-aš-rab-bi-ṭu*, 3, 37; N, 12; R, 6; *mut-taš-ra-bi-ṭu-ti* (v. *tu*), 5, v, 5; *mut-taš-rab-bi-ṭu-ti* (v. *tu*), 5, v, 40; cf. Aš. 3, 27, and X, 2.
šitku, ?: P, 72.
tênu, "to bray": I, 1, *li-te-en-ma*, 9, 133.
tabâlu, "to carry off": I, 1, *ta-ba-li*, B, 21; *ta-bal-ma*, Aš. 12, 63; *lit-bal*, T, r. 13.
tizḳaru, "loud": F, iv, 10.
tiku, "waist," Heb. תָּוֶךְ: DD, 87.
tultu, "worm": Worm, 6, 7, 22.
tamâḫu, "to hold": I, 1, *at-mu-uḫ*, B, 65; *tu-mu-[uḫ]*, G, 11.
tumru, "ashes": N, iii, 8.
tappi . . . , 16, 176.
tappinnu, "dough": T, r. 2, 23.
targullû, U, 35.
turaḫu, "ibex": S, 3, 9; P, 41.
tarâku, "to burst": I, 1, *i-tar-rak*, P, 27.
tarâṣu, "to stretch out straight": I, 1, *tar-ṣa*, DD, 110; *tar-ṣa-at*, DD [57], 78; *tar-ṣu*, 16, 337; V, 14; IV, 1, *lit-ta-ri-iṣ*, 3, 283.
sammu TAR-ṢIR, a plant: 9, 199.
tešu, "destroyer": 16, 41.
tašiltu, "joy": D, iv, 1.